"The principles in this book are great re_____ the business world, how to mentor peo_____ those we mentor. The principles reminded me that sometimes the best thing to do is to listen, learn, and to remind our friends of the importance of balance in one's life. In addition, that opening up and sharing from my own experiences can many times have the most impact."

— DAVID GUTHRIE, chief strategy officer
PTEK Holdings

"*The Heart of Mentoring* is a totally original, surprisingly personal, easy-to-read book. This is a truly timely contribution to sustained and effective mentoring that meets the basic needs of people where they are."

— ROGER BIRKMAN, PH.D., chairman, Birkman International, Inc.

"We spend our lives learning to manage our work, to lead our families, to do our part in making our community run—and to invest the proceeds. Then the accumulated wisdom dies with us! It seldom occurs to us that this wisdom is potentially the biggest, most valuable legacy we have to pass along to another. It isn't too late to invest in another person. Dave Stoddard, in his very practical book, *The Heart of Mentoring*, will both encourage you and show you how to do it!"

— JIM PETERSEN, author, *Living Proof* and *The Insider*

"The governor of my state, Jeb Bush, has often asked me and others to get involved in his mentoring program. . . . I never have because I wasn't sure I knew how. With *The Heart of Mentoring*, I now feel confident that I can make an effective contribution and I'm ready to get started."

— ZOLLIE MAYNARD, Panza, Maurer, Maynard, P.A.
political advisor, attorney, and lobbyist

"*The Heart of Mentoring* is an excellent resource for anyone who would like to leave a lasting legacy. David Stoddard combines how-to practicality with a strong biblical foundation and poignant illustrations. If you have longed to be a mentor or to be mentored, read this informational book."

— CAROL KENT, president, Speak Up Speaker Services; author, *Becoming a Woman of Influence* (NavPress)

"David Stoddard captures the rhythm and essence of a mentoring relationship. I plan to use this book with my corporate clients as a training tool to model the mentoring relationship in leadership development."

— KATHY CARNAHAN, MA, LPC, senior leadership consultant/trainer, CareerLab Inc.

"*The Heart of Mentoring* has had a profound impact on my life, personally and professionally. My work and home relationships are greatly improved, and I have grasped the importance of developing people in my company to their fullest potential. It has reinforced that leadership is a two-way street, made up of win-win relationships in which we learn from each other."

— MICHAEL SVAGDIS, president, Morrison Health Care Food Services

"*The Heart of Mentoring* has given me a good context for conveying what has been going on in my life over the past dozen years and how being mentored has really propelled my career. The book gives me a template for what a mentoring relationship should look like so I can transfer the principles to the people in my division. If developing people and leaders is important to you, the information in this book is invaluable."

— ED CHAFFIN, president, UC eXpress, division of TALX Corporation

THE HEART
of
MENTORING

TEN PROVEN
PRINCIPLES FOR
DEVELOPING PEOPLE
TO THEIR
FULLEST POTENTIAL

DAVID A. STODDARD

WITH ROBERT J. TAMASY

NAVPRESS®

BRINGING TRUTH TO LIFE

OUR GUARANTEE TO YOU

We believe so strongly in the message of our books that we are making this quality guarantee to you. If for any reason you are disappointed with the content of this book, return the title page to us with your name and address and we will refund to you the list price of the book. To help us serve you better, please briefly describe why you were disappointed. Mail your refund request to: NavPress, P.O. Box 35002, Colorado Springs, CO 80935.

The Navigators is an international Christian organization. Our mission is to reach, disciple, and equip people to know Christ and to make Him known through successive generations. We envision multitudes of diverse people in the United States and every other nation who have a passionate love for Christ, live a lifestyle of sharing Christ's love, and multiply spiritual laborers among those without Christ.

NavPress® is the publishing ministry of The Navigators. NavPress publications help believers learn biblical truth and apply what they learn to their lives and ministries. Our mission is to stimulate spiritual formation among our readers.

ISBN 1-57683-401-8

Cover design by Ray Moore
Creative Team: Don Simpson, Amy Spencer, Glynese Northam

Some of the anecdotal illustrations in this book are true to life and are included with the permission of the persons involved. All other illustrations are composites of real situations, and any resemblance to people living or dead is coincidental.

Unless otherwise identified, all Scripture quotations in this publication are taken from the HOLY BIBLE: NEW INTERNATIONAL VERSION® (NIV®). Copyright © 1973, 1978, 1984 by International Bible Society. Used by permission of Zondervan Publishing House. All rights reserved. Other versions used include the *New American Standard Bible* (NASB), © The Lockman Foundation 1960, 1962, 1963, 1968, 1971, 1972, 1973, 1975, 1977; and the *King James Version* (KJV).

Stoddard, David A., 1953-3
  The heart of mentoring : ten proven principles for developing people
to their fullest potential / David A. Stoddard with Robert J. Tamasy.
     p. cm.
Includes bibliographical references.
  ISBN 1-57683-401-8
  1. Mentoring. I. Tamasy, Robert. II. Title.
  BF637.C6S773 2003
  158'.3--dc21
                          2003005257

Printed in the United States of America

4 5 6 7 8 9 10 11 12 / 09 08 07

FOR A FREE CATALOG OF
NAVPRESS BOOKS & BIBLE STUDIES,
CALL 1-800-366-7788 (USA)
OR 1-800-839-4769 (CANADA)

To my wife, Anne, who has stood with me from day one, and to my children, Paul, Aaron, and Sarah. You guys are the best.

CONTENTS

PREFACE

*M*ax graduated from college with simple goals — to get a good job and make a lot of money. He found a job, and the pay was reasonable, but then everything got much more complicated.

"I wanted to conquer the world," he recalls, "but soon I realized things weren't as easy as they first appeared. Success took longer and was more of an ordeal than I had expected. And my dream of an 'ideal job' was shattered by corporate politics and a barrage of mundane tasks."

One morning Max awoke to a collection of questions he could not answer: "Where is the enthusiasm and ambition I used to have? Where is my passion for work and achievement? What am I doing with my life — and why?"

He explored various avenues to find answers, including interviews, seminars, and books, and he gathered as many ideas as possible. But his feelings of disappointment and diminished motivation persisted. With his life in such a muddle, he wondered how he could ever consider getting married and raising a family.

Bordering on despair, Max approached an older man who mentored others and asked for his help. The two men began to meet once a week and discovered they shared similar mindsets, interests, and goals. A strong bond soon formed, and the weeks grew into months.

The mentor did not load Max down with advice and assignments. Instead, he listened, asked questions, and made occasional suggestions. He offered insights from experience and demonstrated a willingness to be there when Max needed him. Slowly—but unquestionably—Max found answers to his questions, including the deeper, more profound ones about the whats and whys of his life.

Today his enthusiasm for work has returned, and he has attained a measure of success. He and his wife recently had their first child and approach family life with great optimism. Most of all, Max has discovered a sense of purpose and vision that energizes his life, in the workplace and outside it.

There are millions of men and women like Max who are desperately searching for direction and meaning as they rush to keep up with our fast-paced world. For many of them, a mentor could make all the difference—but not just any mentor. They need the kind of mentor who sees them as multidimensional, dynamic people with needs extending far beyond tasks and responsibilities. Such a mentor understands that we each are a unique mix of mind, body, spirit, and emotion.

Mentoring is commonplace today, particularly in the world of work, but too often it focuses solely on behavior and skills. Such a focus is helpful, but in *The Heart of Mentoring* I address a greater need: mentoring that deals with the whole person, seeking to encourage change and develop people from the inside out.

My hope is to stir and inspire the hearts of readers, creating in them a passion for mentoring. For this reason and others, my focus is not on methodology, but on foundational, life-changing principles that work in mentoring, marriage, family life, and virtually all other relationships. If you focus on these principles—whether in formal or informal mentoring—the necessary skills and methods will "come alive."

These principles have changed my life and the lives of hundreds of men and women I know, and they can change your life as well. Here is just a sampling of the principles I will discuss in the chapters that follow (a list of all ten appears at the end of the book):

+ Mentoring is a journey that requires perseverance.
+ Mentoring includes helping mentoring partners to determine their priorities, uncover their passions, and honestly address their pain.
+ Mentoring concentrates on the needs of the one being mentored, not on the agenda of the mentor.
+ Mentoring focuses on changing people from the inside out, not the outside in.
+ Mentoring involves the spiritual side of a person, not just the physical, mental, and emotional aspects.
+ Mentoring is one of the best ways to have a significant personal impact on society, even for generations.

In some writings, the terms *coaching* (or *executive coaching*) and *mentoring* are used interchangeably, but I see substantial differences between them and will be focusing on mentoring here. Although I utilize executive coaching as well as mentoring in my work, I'm afraid the idea of coaching in business has become a fad. Coaching typically is skills driven, short term, and focused on behavior, while mentoring is relationship oriented, has a long-term scope, and is wholistic, meaning it is broad enough to address facets of the whole person, not just a narrow slice of the individual's life. In fact, a coaching dimension can be included in the mentoring relationship to address specific areas of need or concern.

You will find that most of the examples I use involve men. I have found great value in men mentoring men and women mentoring women. For formal mentoring relationships that focus exclusively on tasks and projects, this may not be an issue, but in mentoring the whole person I have found that I cannot relate to a lot of the issues that women face, and women cannot relate to a lot of men's issues. Men draw great benefit from intense, no-holds-barred time with other men in mentoring, and women need the same kind of time with other women. But the principles — the big ideas — apply equally for both genders.

Also, because spirituality is a very important issue in the workplace today, it's one that comes up in mentoring relationships with surprising frequency. Personally, after years of study and searching, I determined that the source of my own spirituality would be the Bible. I found it the most helpful and relevant tool for establishing a standard from which to build a complete worldview. So from time to time I will cite principles from the Bible to clarify some of my thoughts on mentoring. I hope you will find this beneficial.

As we walk through these pages together, I hope to convince you that there is really only one type of person in this world: the person who needs to be a "mentored mentor." I have concluded that each of us needs mentoring and we also need to mentor others. The people I know who are getting the most out of life — and putting the most back into it — are those who are committed to this mutual mentoring process. This is where true fulfillment lies. Indeed, I have found that this is one of the greatest joys you can experience. I invite you to join me on this journey!

David A. Stoddard
Atlanta, Georgia

ACKNOWLEDGMENTS

*F*irst, I want to thank my mentors: Dave Hill, who unselfishly invested in my life, and Jim Petersen, who not only continues to mentor me, but also has been a treasured friend who has inspired, consoled, and reassured me every step of the way.

Many thanks also for the help and support of the following people, without whom this book would not have been possible:

My friends at NavPress/Piñon Press: Kent Wilson, for his inspiration in writing this book; Toben Heim, who always fires me up; and Don Simpson, for his encouragement and humble spirit. Bob Tamasy, for his great gift of communicating my heart in his writing. My wife, Anne, for her great editing. And Roger Birkman, whose life is a tremendous model for me.

Thanks also must go to my many friends and supporters both past and present, without whom our call in Leader's Legacy to develop the leader in people through mentoring could not be fulfilled: John and Cissy Persichetti, David and Caroline Abday, Bill Amick, Wick and Margie Ashburn, Jim Bailey, David and Amy Barrs, Paul and Liz Baum, Ron Bell, Jim and Shari Campbell, Alex and Chris Cann, Steve and Kimberly Capizzi, Steve and Nancy Carley, Christopher Cochran, Tom Comsudes, Bob and Karen Copley, Jeff and Elaine Davis, Lee and Shewjen Davis, Paul and Joanie DeBolt, David and Cantey Deeter, Steve and Barb Denbow, Rob and Sheryl Erickson, Dave Fonseca, Mark and Dianne Fonseca,

Mark and Martha Fouraker, Paul Franklin, Jerry and Jan Geiger, Matt and Tasha Given, David and Lydia Guthrie, David and Doreen Hamilton, Mike Hammer, Jim Hancock, Doug Harms, Jim and Darcy Harper, Mark and Sherry Harrell, Ken and Denise Henley, Ted and Gladys Hubbard, Tom and Geri Jablonski, Ken Johnson, Scott and Beth Johnson, John and Mary Keefe, Mike and Selena Keenan, Joe Klass, Brian Koch, Lincoln Kokaram, Joe and Ella Koscik, Gerald and Lannie Lambert, Mike and Judy Landry, Kevin and Nikki Lott, Mike and Carol Marker, Glenn and Chrysan McCoin, Chris and Sherry McLatcher, Derrick and Karen Merck, Ted Noble, Gerry Organ, Mark Palmer, Larry and Sharon Pearson, Steve and Toria Peterson, Mark Pollard, Jim and Lucia Rayburn, Carter and Beth Reames, David Rees, Kevin and Gail Ring, Dave Scott, Cy and Dee Smith, Rob and Kim Smith, Jon and Libby Soderberg, Barry and Lori Spencer, Dale and Yvonne Spencer, Deane and Beverly Stokes Sr., Deane Stokes Jr., Terry and Lori Terhune, Bill and Eloise Terry, Brad and Christine Thomas, Jim and Sandy Underwood, Don and Kate VanVolkenburg, George and Therese Walker, Mark and Becky West, Mark Whitmire, Todd Young, and Fred and Rosemary Zillich.

I'm also thankful for the impact of my sister, Eve, and my brothers, Ted and John, on my life. Since my high school years, they have always been there for me during good times, and even more importantly, during the tough times of my life. Finally, to my dad (who has passed from this earth) and my mom: Thank you for everything, for loving all of us and giving of yourselves.

A TALE OF TWO MENTORS

*T*wo young men eagerly anticipated meeting with their mentors for the first time. One of them would find the experience to be the best of times; for the other, it would feel more like the worst of times.

Kyle was in his early thirties, a rising executive with a software startup company in a major city. Outwardly, he appeared self-assured and successful, the type of person envied by his peers. From their perspective, he had it "all together." But inside, the real Kyle felt nothing but turmoil. He was nursing the emotional bruises of a broken engagement. His personal finances were in shambles; despite a very comfortable income, he had accumulated debts totaling into five figures. And even though his job was both challenging and personally rewarding, Kyle had grown weary of his day-to-day routine. *What do I want to do with my life?* was a question he often asked himself, but he did not know where to look for the answer.

Perhaps it would help to find a mentor to guide me through some of these issues, Kyle reasoned. Finally, he mustered up the courage to approach Walt, a man about ten years older, and ask whether he would be interested in helping him through a mentoring relationship.

"I didn't know Walt real well," Kyle says, "but I had observed some character qualities in him that I admired. He was more mature and obviously had already worked through many of the issues I was facing.

He seemed quiet and laid-back, sometimes even a little distant, but from listening to him in discussions, I knew he was deep, well read, and thoughtful. I could see how he tried to integrate different ideas from influential writers and apply them in practical ways, and since I'm that kind of person, too, I thought we would hit it off well."

When approached about serving as a mentor, "Walt jumped all over it," Kyle recalls. "I could see that it meant a lot for someone to ask him to become his mentor. He seemed pleased, confident, and receptive. I felt good as well, certain that I had gone to the right man for mentoring."

That certainty quickly began to fade, however. "When we got together for the first time, I came with no agenda," Kyle says. "I was looking to Walt for leadership, expecting him to say something like, 'Okay, here's what we're going to do.' But right from the beginning, he seemed to struggle with defining how our relationship would take shape. Finally, he gave me a book and suggested that I read it, and we could discuss it each week when we met in his office. We did that, but even in that initial meeting, I worried that we might be going nowhere. Something was missing. I just didn't know what."

What Kyle had been hoping for was a trusting relationship with open, honest interaction with his mentor on a variety of topics, both business and personal. Instead, he wrestled with having to complete the reading assignments, feeling he was expected to come ready for the next session, much like being enrolled in a college class.

"I don't think Walt intended to do so, but he made me feel pressured. I felt guilty when I would arrive for a meeting unprepared — as I often did. That put me under extra stress, which I did not need or want at the time."

Before long, Kyle began to purposely look for ways to cancel the meetings. "I just felt so inadequate, like every week I was letting Walt down. And when we did meet, it wasn't what I was looking for. I had thought that with his years of experience and insight, Walt could show me how to reach my goals faster, and that through sharing from his life, he could provide me with a kind of road map to follow: What were the disciplines, the things you do and don't do, to get ahead in business — and in life?

"I had also envisioned a relationship that would be mutually beneficial, a win-win situation in which we could learn from one another. But we never got to the point where we started to get to know each other on a deeper, personal level. I never felt invited to enter into his life and world. And I never felt comfortable meeting in his office — like I was intruding into his busy schedule. I thought it would have been great to just hang out together, even at a restaurant, simply getting to know each other better, but that never happened."

Eventually, the "mentoring" relationship dissolved and they stopped meeting, although to this day, Kyle holds deep respect for Walt and still considers him a friend.

Like Kyle, Brian took the initiative to find a mentor. He was twenty-eight, not yet married, and an attorney with a law firm that specialized in the transportation industry. For him, the catalyst for seeking a mentoring relationship was attending a men's conference on personal spirituality. He had felt challenged to take a serious look at the spiritual dimension of his life, thinking it could provide a sense of balance that he lacked, but having no idea how to go about that.

At the suggestion of one of the speakers at the conference, Brian started going to a series of follow-up meetings, but after several weeks he decided he wanted more personalized attention. After one of the meetings, he asked Steve, a regular participant, if he knew of anyone he could talk with one-on-one about some spiritual questions he had.

Brian recalls what happened next: "Steve looked at me, paused for a couple of moments, and then said, 'Hey, I can do that. I like to work with guys like you. Would you mind meeting with me?' 'No, I wouldn't mind at all. That would be great,' I replied."

Steve, who had been mentoring younger men for years, had casually noticed how Brian interacted at the meetings and had already decided that if the young attorney showed an interest in being mentored, he would offer to help.

"Judging from Brian's comments — in the meetings and in casual conversations we had before and afterward — I sensed that his life was in chaos," Steve comments. "Soon after we started to meet, it became clear that he wasn't sure about much of anything in his life. Attorneys are trained to act as if they are in command of any situation. Who wants to go to someone who admits, 'Gee, I don't have any idea what we should do!'? But Brian was struggling, professionally and personally, and desperately needed to find some direction for his life."

So while their meetings initially had a spiritual focus, the two men eventually talked about virtually every aspect of their lives. For instance, when he met Steve, Brian had been dating a young woman for several years but was uncertain whether to pursue marriage. Talking about his concerns, Brian realized they were hardly insurmountable, and he and Larissa now have been married for five years and have two children.

Steve, who had enjoyed many successful years in business, also helped Brian work through a variety of career-related issues, ranging from whether to take the risk of starting his own law firm to how to resolve some very difficult personnel problems.

"At this point in our relationship," Brian says, "I can't think of any area of my life that Steve hasn't touched. But the thing I like best is that when I go to him for advice, even now, he's not quick to tell me what he thinks I should do. It's more that he helps me to find the answer myself. If it's a situation he can relate to, Steve tells me about his own experience. He also throws out a lot of questions, probing for pertinent information and asking if I have thought about factors that might have a bearing on my decision. He likes to help me narrow down to a couple of choices, but then he keeps asking questions until I reach my own conclusion.

"Frankly, if he were to give me quick solutions, I might not accept them very readily. His process of raising questions helps me to think things through and, once I find a resolution, I feel a sense of owner-ship — that it's my decision, not something forced on me."

Steve explains why he has found this approach so useful through his years of mentoring: "Many young people today are carrying a lot of clutter around with them: broken relationships, no clear-cut set of values, unfulfilled goals and desires, disoriented careers, and a general lack of purpose. Rather than trying to fix things quickly, I find it's much more effective to challenge their thinking, to get them to work through the whats and whys and hows of the issues they are facing."

According to Brian, one reason the mentoring relationship grew so strong is that Steve made him feel a part of his life. "From the start, he was real, nothing phony about him," Brian says. "And then he invited me into his home, opening up his family life to me. It was great to see him living out the principles he talked about with me when we would meet. To let me into his private life took trust on his part, and trust begets trust. My trust in him increased tremendously."

Clearly, Brian's experience in being mentored was far more grati-fying than Kyle's, but as commentator Paul Harvey likes to declare, in both cases there is "the rest of the story."

While Kyle's first experience in being mentored fell far short of what he had envisioned, he did not give up on the concept of mentoring entirely. Not long after he and Walt parted ways, Kyle began meeting with another man, Jack. The contrast between the two mentors was huge in Kyle's estimation.

"After my first experience, I felt a bit gun-shy," Kyle says, "but still wanted to find someone who could mentor me. Jack was another man I looked up to, so I asked if he would meet with me. He caught me off guard when he agreed to do so, on one condition: that I would give him permission to probe into any area of my life and that I would be honest in my answers, as he intended to be with me. That was an intimidating request, but when Jack started talking openly with me about his own struggles, his vulnerability freed me to be more open with him.

"Another thing I liked about Jack was that he came with little or no expectation of me, and his agenda was wide open. He was just sincerely interested in being able to help me in whatever way he could."

Over time, Kyle became a member of Jack's extended family, spending hundreds of hours in his home, observing his mentor's life in action, not just in words. "Jack and his wife would often have several guys over at a time," Kyle says, "but it was rarely to get together just for a meeting. There was always an element of family involved: building relationships over a meal, playing games, watching a basketball game, or simply sitting around and talking about anything that came to mind."

The guidance and support Kyle had hoped to find with Walt finally came through his relationship with Jack. "It's not that Walt didn't help me at all, because he did. But spending time with Jack really put me on a fast track, professionally and personally. I really grew through Jack's mentoring. If I were to sum up in just a word or two the impact he had on my life, I would say it was life changing."

As for Brian, he and Steve maintain a strong friendship today, more than seven years after they started their mentoring relationship, and they still meet frequently for breakfast or lunch to catch up on each other's lives.

"Growing up," says Brian, "if I thought of mentoring at all, I envisioned it as a six-month project where someone meets with you for a while and then goes away. It hasn't been that way with Steve. I never felt like I was a project with him, but rather that I was a part of his life and that our time together was as important to Steve as it was to me."

After discovering firsthand the benefits of having a mentor, Brian has begun mentoring men himself over the past several years. "I really didn't go out 'recruiting' someone to mentor. It just started happening. One guy and then a couple of others — all about my age — sought me out for advice. Now we meet regularly and I try to be a help to each of them. All I'm doing is communicating what Steve has communicated to me over the years.

"One fellow and I had been riding bikes together for a long time, and he began to ask me about some issues he was facing at work and in his marriage. Then he started to ask me about spiritual things, and eventually he opened other areas of his life to me as well. Our wives have become good friends, and I think we are all helping each other. This experience has been incredible!

"But if Steve had not started mentoring me years ago — modeling it for me — I know I wouldn't be mentoring others today. I would just be out there floundering around, trying to earn a paycheck and somehow find time to spend with my family. I definitely wouldn't have the passion to help others if I hadn't learned what it meant in my own life."

The names and minor details in this "tale of two mentors" have been changed, but both stories are factual. The comments from the men being mentored appear just as they expressed them. And these accounts are indicative of the state of mentoring today: Everyone agrees about the need for it, but too few people are engaged in this process — especially in its truest, most meaningful sense.

The vastly different experiences Kyle and Brian had with their first mentors can be attributed to one simple, self-evident truth: All mentors are not created equal. But the difference for these two was not so much the personalities, abilities, or comparative life experiences of their mentors. It was more a matter of two men with a sharply different understanding (or misunderstanding) of the role of a mentor and what a mentoring relationship should look like.

There is an old saying that affirms an obvious yet profound reality: People don't know what they don't know. This certainly applies to mentoring. For instance, Walt, the first mentor we met, may have sincerely believed he was mentoring Kyle by providing him with material for discussion. But he missed the point entirely. In seeking a mentor, Kyle wasn't just wanting information. He was looking for a helpful relationship, for someone who could provide a road map — or a compass of sorts — to show him how to find his way in the chaotic world around him. Kyle wanted answers for the everyday struggles he was facing in both his personal and professional life. He just didn't know how to ask for it — and Walt didn't know how to provide it.

Never has the need for mentoring been greater. Constant change in our society has spawned constant uncertainty. And this constant uncertainty creates a yearning to connect with someone who can provide comfort as well as answers. In a chaotic world — whether it's in the workplace, the home, or the community — it helps to find a person who has already been at the stage of life where you are and has learned through the trials of life, as well as its triumphs.

Most of what takes place today under the guise of mentoring tends to be based on a task or a position, rather than on developing the whole person. While the concept of mentoring is gaining more and more acceptance, particularly in business, it typically takes a formal, programmatic approach. The mentor and the one to be mentored each submit an application. The mentoring program coordinator determines which mentor to match with which "mentoree," aligning needs with experience and expertise. Then both individuals receive training in how to conduct themselves to maximize results from this mentoring relationship. If it sounds sterile, that's because it is. That's the way "mentoring" is normally done in the world of business, but it's hardly the best way, particularly in a long-range sense.

It's time to bid a not-so-fond farewell to this old paradigm and move into the twenty-first century. We need to redefine what mentoring truly is and then to redesign how we go about doing it.

In many cases, people today who call themselves mentors are merely going through the motions. They are motivated by guilt or necessity, not by a passion for making a difference in the lives of others — and that is the crux of the problem. Mentoring is not a matter of skills and behavior; it's a matter of the heart.

The heart of mentoring is helping people to reach their fullest potential in life, not just to teach them how to perform a task the right way, to carry out the responsibilities of a position, or to acquire knowledge, even though those obviously have value. And we can't separate our professional lives from our private lives; if our private lives suffer, they will affect our professional lives, and vice versa.

In classic discussions of mentoring, the center of attention usually is the mentor, not the one being mentored. These discussions focus on the mentor imparting wisdom and knowledge in a particular area of expertise to the person being mentored, but little is said about relationships. I'm convinced that people are tired of theory, tired of learning concepts that seem disconnected from real life.

That's why I have enjoyed several viewings of *Finding Forrester*, a movie starring Sean Connery. It's a moving drama about an aging white novelist, William Forrester, who unintentionally develops a kinship with a keen black teenager, Jamal Wallace. But it's far more than a story about how friendships can transcend age and racial differences. At its heart, *Finding Forrester* is a story about the impact mentoring can have on the lives of both people involved.

As we meet Forrester and Wallace, it becomes evident that both are looking for something, only they don't know what. Forrester, a recluse who once wrote a Pulitzer Prize–winning novel, recognizes a void in his life. Wallace, a talented basketball player, is struggling to find an outlet for another passion: writing. Over time, they discover they can help one another. Forrester becomes Wallace's writing mentor, but in the process, Wallace teaches him some valuable lessons as well.

Finding Forrester is fiction, but through the years I have experienced and observed many mentoring relationships that have had a similar impact. If you're like me, you want to learn principles of mentoring that work, but you want to encounter them through examples of real people in real-life situations. Principles communicated through story have a more profound effect on people and their lives than ideas presented outside the scope of human experience. I have found stories and principles from the Bible to be great examples of this.

So, over the chapters that follow, I will unwrap this new paradigm, this new "worldview" of mentoring, utilizing illustrations from my own life and from the lives of people I have been privileged to know. We will see how mentoring is a process, not a program or a project. It's a journey that requires great patience, persistence, and perseverance. It also is a relationship that often endures for a long time — even many years — because when the mentor and the mentored engage in a life-to-life exchange, they learn and benefit from one another. In my experience, change in the life of another person almost always is a reflection of changes going on in my own life.

We will see how mentoring involves helping others to discover and pursue their passions, recognize and deal with their pain, and sort out their priorities. And while we are pondering all these Ps, let me suggest another one. In considering the mentoring relationship, several associates and I have debated over what would be the best term to use for the object of the mentor's attention. *Mentoree* was one possibility, but it almost sounds like some kind of dessert topping. *Mentee* sounded too much like someone with psychological problems. The most commonly used term, *protégé*, has a condescending sound to it and just isn't the kind of word that you pack into the average vocabulary.

Therefore, after much discussion, we settled on the word *partner*. This term seems right because mentoring is not something you do *to* someone, but *with* someone. The image we are trying to dispense with is that of the supposed expert or authority who stoops to confer a measure of favor upon a lesser individual. While experiences, expertise, and knowledge may differ greatly between the mentor and partner, the best mentoring relationship results when participants view each other as equals or partners in working toward a common goal: personal growth and achievement.

As I will explain in chapter 1, I first became involved in mentoring in 1979 when a man came alongside me and willingly shared his life with a very troubled and confused young man. About four years later, I began my first halting attempts at mentoring others, experiencing some notable failures before achieving any measure of success. But in almost every case, the approach was that we were equals in the process, fellow participants who were going to learn from each other.

So I like the term *mentoring partner*. When I mentor someone, I come prepared — and expecting — to learn, not just to teach and advise. As I step into another person's world and he steps into mine, we begin to see the world afresh, from different perspectives. Neither of us will ever be the same.

Now I invite you to step into my world for awhile so I can show you how I arrived at my conclusions about mentoring and why I believe they can, without any exaggeration, have a profound, life-changing impact on your life — and on the legacy you one day will leave behind.

CHAPTER 1

IT STARTS WITH THE HEART

· ·

PRINCIPLE #1: EFFECTIVE MENTORS UNDERSTAND
THAT LIVING IS ABOUT GIVING.

· ·

One morning a few months ago, I was sitting on a wooden platform at the foot of a waterfall in northeastern Georgia. I had several books and magazines with me, as well as two notebooks and a backpack filled with pens, bottled water, energy bars, insect repellant, and other supplies that a serious author needs for a productive day. The sound of the water crashing down the rocks to the churning pool below and then rushing along its downstream course was crisp and invigorating.

I had been diligently researching and writing down my thoughts for about an hour when another man climbed down the stairs to the platform so he also could enjoy the view. After a minute or two he turned and, noticing the materials sprawled around me, asked what I was working on. I told him I was in the midst of writing a book on mentoring.

"No kidding? I'm part of a mentoring program myself," the man replied. He explained it was an optional activity for government employees in his particular state. His department worked in inner-city communities to help in solving problems, and he had decided to

CHAPTER ONE

take advantage of the opportunity to designate one hour a week—
with pay—for mentoring a young inner-city person.

Having observed that so many teenagers, regardless of where
they live, seem to lack direction, I thought this mentoring concept
sounded like a good idea. Being curious about this man's motivation,
I asked why he had decided to make himself available as a mentor.

"Well, I would like to help them to achieve a better life," he
answered.

"That's great!" I responded, before asking, "Do you find it really
fulfilling? Do you love doing it?"

"Not really," he admitted with a shake of his head. "I have a family and I'm extremely busy, and sometimes the young people don't follow through on what I ask them to do. So it can be frustrating.
Sometimes it seems like a waste of time."

"Then why do you do it?"

He paused for a moment and then commented, "Well, I think
mentoring can help solve some community problems. But mostly, I
think, because it's just a part of my job."

Wow! "It's just a part of my job." Without knowing it, that man
standing alongside the busy waterfall had just summed up the general state of mentoring today. He was involved in it, and I commend
him for that. But he certainly did not have the heart for it or a clear
understanding of what genuine mentoring is all about. He had
started out with high expectations, envisioning how these young
people would welcome his advice and words of wisdom and then
eagerly begin to apply them. When that didn't happen and he didn't
see results fast enough, his good intentions began to fade and mentoring turned into just another line on his job description.

This government employee is not alone. Typically, much of the mentoring I have seen and experienced in the business and professional world is treated as a program or project. There is a certain value in this, to be sure, but at the core, mentoring must be a matter of the heart. Whether you take an informal or formal approach, if your heart is not in it, you cannot be effective. Trying to do something when your heart isn't in it feels cumbersome and becomes a chore, not an activity you enjoy and look forward to doing. At best, you go through the motions; deep down your sentiments might be like a friend of mine who says, "I'd rather eat a bug."

Effective mentoring begins with the heart, motivated from the inside, then manifests itself outwardly — not the other way around. If our mentoring focuses only on expected outcomes, we inevitably forget that the central focus of mentoring is the people involved. More than just a sound business practice, mentoring is really a stewardship issue. It's an opportunity to give of ourselves — our experiences, our expertise, and our gifts — and take advantage of opportunities to help someone (to borrow from the U.S. Army slogan) be all that they can be. Those who mentor from the heart have discovered a foundational principle: The secret to living is giving.

To help you get a picture of what I mean, let me start by telling you about how mentoring became a central part of who I am today.

PRINCIPLES MORE EASILY CAUGHT
THAN TAUGHT

It all began in 1979, when a businessman named Dave Hill invited me to lunch. At the time, I was working with my brother in a construction company that we had started, and I was flattered to have a successful businessman with so much credibility ask to spend some time with me.

To be honest, back then I would not have been on anyone's list of potential role models in the business world. I didn't know how much it showed, but I was greatly confused about what I wanted to do in my life. Financially, I was a wreck and didn't have much hope of getting things turned around. So, when Dave offered to meet with me, I couldn't believe it.

Talking with him over lunch was incredible. There I was, sitting across from a man who represented the kind of person I wanted to become one day: accomplished, confident, in control of his finances, and exhibiting a clear sense of what his life was about. He seemed at peace with himself and life, and showed contentment and an obvious sense of purpose — everything I lacked. Meeting with him felt intimidating at first, but Dave's interest and genuineness eventually enabled me to relax and loosen up.

We had a great time together, but after I left the restaurant, do you know what I did? I didn't get fired up, excited that I had found someone who was willing to mentor me. It was just the opposite. I sat in my car, without turning on the ignition, as tears welled up in my eyes. I felt certain — I just knew — that once Dave saw who I really was and the mess I had made of my life, he wouldn't want to meet with me anymore. Why would he want to waste his time? I may have looked good on the outside — I had to do this to survive — but on the inside I was filled with confusion and despair.

But I was wrong. We had scheduled an appointment for the next week and when I arrived at the restaurant, Dave was there. As we talked, he asked me a lot of direct questions, but not once did I feel that he was judging me. To my amazement, Dave accepted me for me. He met me right where I was.

The interesting thing about Dave was how open he was with me, sharing very candidly from his own life. He taught me principles he had discovered through experience, showing that he could relate to the struggles I was facing. While he was far ahead of me both professionally and personally, I learned he had areas of his life in which he still struggled. Using his own stories, Dave demonstrated that he wasn't talking theoretically but was offering valuable insights that he knew worked in real life. Often as we met, I would sit there and think, "Man, I hope I can be like Dave one day!" Knowing he had confronted and learned how to deal with challenges of his own gave me some hope.

I'll never forget the times we would meet and I would tell Dave about my latest problem, whatever it happened to be. He would lean back in his chair, flash his kind and understanding smile, and assure me, "Dave, you're in a great position!" At first I thought he was crazy. *What do you mean—a great position?* I would think to myself. *I've got a big problem!* But as we talked through each situation, he would always point me toward a solution. Slowly, through his mentoring, my life started to take a positive turn. Appreciating how much his help meant in my life, the desire grew in my heart to one day be able to come alongside someone else in the same way.

YOU HAVE TO START SOMEWHERE

In 1983, with some trepidation and a lot of faulty ideas, I took my first steps on the path to becoming a mentor. I began to meet with one man. To be honest, I did all the wrong things. At least that's how it seems to me now. It was so bad that I can't even remember the guy's name! But I was young and had to start somewhere.

My biggest problem was that I approached mentoring with an

agenda. I focused on changing the other guy's behavior, expecting him to complete the assignments I gave him to do. (Somewhere along the line, I forgot how I had often failed to do many of the assignments my friend Dave had given me.) In this initial attempt at mentoring, I could see that the young man's primary objective was to get to know me, to become acquainted with someone a little more seasoned than him, and to learn from my experiences. But when he would show up for a meeting without having done the assignment, I would frown and let him know I wasn't pleased. Basically, I made him feel like a failure.

After a total of three meetings, we never met again. In retrospect, I can't blame him; we have enough opportunities in life to fail without meeting voluntarily with someone who wants to reinforce our negative feelings. Determining that mentoring hadn't brought the results I had expected, I concluded it wasn't for me and I wouldn't do it anymore. It took me a while to realize it, but my attitude toward mentoring had been totally self-centered, not other-centered. Like the man I encountered by the waterfall, I felt mentoring was a good thing to do, but I had not yet acquired the heart for real mentoring. I still had not realized that it was all about what I was willing to give, not what I wanted to receive.

You may have heard the story of the prominent leader known for his business savvy who was asked to explain his secret of success. "How did you acquire your wisdom?" he was asked. "By making good decisions," was his response. "Well, how do you learn to make good decisions?" "By making bad decisions," he replied. I can relate to that. My early mentoring experiences were fraught with mistakes and poor decisions, but with time I discovered that failure can serve as a wonderful teacher.

Finally, by reflecting on how Dave had mentored me, I resolved simply to model for other men what he had demonstrated for me. Recalling our times together, I remembered that my unfinished assignments never bothered him. And it had not been assignments that had begun to turn my life around anyway. It was the fact that Dave was there, ready to offer comfort and encouragement when needed, along with hope for a very frightened mentoring partner.

One of Dave's goals had been to bring me to a point where I was prepared to work with others. His impact during that stage of my young adult life is incalculable. He helped me to find the balance my life needed so desperately, provided much-needed insight for my struggling business, showed me how to climb out of a deep hole of debt, and stood by me as I met and then prepared to marry the woman of my dreams. Most of all, Dave reflected the joy and fulfill-ment that comes from "giving your life away" — investing time, energy, and genuine care in another person.

Under his wing, I grew from a child to a peer, developing my own heart for mentoring others. Dave and I remain close friends to this day, although our relationship eventually took a different shape. I did not realize it as we met week after week, month after month, that he was preparing me for a totally new stage in my life, a time when a new mentor would begin to take me further along in the journey as I addressed some complex career issues. But we will save that story for another chapter in this book.

It has been more than twenty years since my first experience in mentoring. Contrary to my impression at the outset, I have consis-tently found what an incredible opportunity it is to mentor young people, many of them struggling with issues similar to those that confronted me when I first started meeting with Dave. The best part is that every time I mentor someone, I feel I'm learning a lot, too;

sometimes it's like we are mentoring each other.

At this point, you might be thinking something like, *Dave, that's a nice story and I'm glad for you, but why should I bother to get involved in mentoring?* Well, I'm glad you asked. The answer is simple. As Dave Hill told me so many times during the years we met together, "There is no greater joy than giving your life away."

To be honest, when he first said this to me, I didn't believe him, but over the years I have come to appreciate the profound truth of that statement. Robert Lupton, who for more than twenty years has directed a nonprofit organization in Atlanta that is dedicated to helping and equipping the urban poor to live productive, self-sustaining lives, has reached this amazing conclusion: "The greatest poverty is the inability to give." Lupton has discovered that a key component of providing a sense of self-worth and meaning to people in poor circumstance is being able to turn the tables and enable them to become givers rather than always being recipients.

If what Lupton says is true — that the greatest poverty is the inability to give — then it would seem that the contrast would also be true: The greatest *wealth* is the *ability to give*. That's why I have realized that my friend Dave is right. There really is nothing like giving your life away.

One of the major reasons many people are not giving their lives away and experiencing joy and fulfillment in helping others is that they are too engrossed in themselves. But there are consequences of excessive self-interest, including stress and misery. This happens because self-centeredness is opposed to how we have been designed to need one another, serving as mutual sources of support. In his book *Stewardship*, Peter Block expresses the idea this way: "The antidote to self-interest is to commit and to find a cause. To commit to something outside of ourselves. To be a part of creating something we care about so we can endure the sacrifice, risk and adventure that commitment entails. This is the deeper meaning of service."[1]

In the post–September 11 world, we have seen a growing comprehension of this truth. Recent surveys show that these tragedies, which helped each of us to gain a deeper understanding of the value and brevity of life, have prompted Americans to begin refocusing their lives more outwardly. For instance, about three out of every four people polled indicate that helping others holds far greater significance to them now than before 9-11. At the other side of the spectrum, "making lots of money" remains a paramount concern for only about 20 percent of those surveyed.

More than 75 percent of those responding state that spending more time with their families has grown in importance, and approximately two-thirds have a heightened desire to serve the country in some manner. Isn't it interesting how the leading responses point to people shifting their focus from themselves to the needs of others?

Jesus of Nazareth, who demonstrated great expertise in the area of mentoring, strongly espoused this premise in statements about the importance and value of giving from one's life. For instance, he said, "Greater love has no one than this, that he lay down his life for his friends" (John 15:13). Jesus said something else that is even more familiar to us: "It is more blessed to give than to receive" (Acts 20:35). Giving, as so many people have said and as has proved true in my own experience, is an important aspect of everyday life.

There are many avenues for giving to and serving others, but in terms of long-term investment of self, I can't think of a greater cause than giving our lives away to others through mentoring. Many people I know have arrived at the same conclusion. In fact, some business leaders, once they have sampled the rewards of mentoring others, have reordered their lives and schedules to ensure they keep time free to serve as mentors.

The first time I experienced any degree of success in mentoring was in 1984. I was teaching a Bible class for young adults, mostly business and professional people. One fellow was sitting right up front, but I could tell he was not relating to anything I had to say. Don obviously had no interest. But to my surprise, after the meeting he came up to me and for whatever reason began to tell me about some personal challenges he was facing. His wife had just left him, he was struggling with an alcohol problem, and overall his life was in disarray. Someone had given him a self-help book that I was familiar with, but he was having trouble getting into it.

"Would you like me to go through it with you?" I asked, the words tumbling out of my mouth almost before I was aware of thinking them. Don's eyes lit up and he responded, "Would you?" He couldn't believe that someone would be willing to spend some time with him.

We met at a restaurant for the first time later that week and continued meeting almost weekly for several months. We never really got into the self-help book. What this young man needed most was someone who would listen to him, show that he cared, and offer some helpful comments every once in a while. Over the months, Don and I embarked on a mentoring journey that saw his life change. It really wasn't my doing; I was simply an instrument, a resource to help him get started on the right course to begin repairing his life. I certainly had not yet grasped the dynamics of mentoring. It was just evident that this man was hurting, and I was willing to be there to help in whatever way I could.

I see similarities between mentoring and raising children. When my wife, Anne, and I first started having kids, we viewed them as they were: helpless, needy, crying much of the time, making messes. Yet there was not one moment when Anne and I would have hesitated to lay our lives down for them if that were necessary. These little lives were so precious, there wasn't anything we wouldn't do for them. We accepted them at whatever stages they were, realizing that one day they wouldn't be as helpless or as needy. They wouldn't make as many messes, and when they did, they would learn to clean them up themselves.

In mentoring, we need a similar passion for people. Just because they are adults doesn't mean they won't have issues in their lives that need to be addressed — especially when they are young. They also are hungry and in need of help. They want to learn. They are looking for answers. They need caring mentors who will be there for them. As my friend Jim Hancock says, "It's almost like they are asking, 'How can I steal the experience and insight older people have?' while older people are asking, 'How can I give away what I have learned through the years?'"

GIVING FOR THE RIGHT REASONS

But a key to giving — whether it involves material goods or the time and energy required in a mentoring relationship — is not to give because of guilt or obligation. The Bible talks about giving "not reluctantly or under compulsion" (2 Corinthians 9:7), but cheerfully and eagerly. Recently, I met with a man who is noted for his philanthropy. His affluence has enabled him to give generously to a variety of worthy causes. As I talked with him, it became clear that he has a real passion for helping people.

So I asked him, "Are you getting any joy from your philanthropy?" He looked at me, slowly shook his head, and replied, "No, I do events for organizations and give away a lot of my money, but no one has asked me to get involved hands-on." Then he added with a note of sadness, "And that's what I'd love to do."

From the time we are infants, we have a built-in need and desire for significant relationships. It's just there — we don't have to ask for it. It's part of the package. And this need for relationships doesn't stop once we have grown to adulthood. The characteristics of our relationships change, of course, but we need them just as much.

Deepening this feeling of need is the fact that most of us have lost our sense of community. In generations past, people were raised and remained in the same towns or neighborhoods. Their significant relationships were virtually guaranteed. Today broken homes and splintered families have caused an unbelievable fragmentation of relationships. Compounding this problem is the fact that in cities like my hometown of Atlanta, people are very transient, moving to other areas so quickly they don't have time to put down any meaningful roots.

A by-product of this loss of community is a lack of clarity and focus among young adults, particularly the twenty-somethings. They lack role models to point the way. They also experience little peace and contentment, and have few clues for where to find them. They are afraid of failing, of not experiencing lives that are worthwhile and rewarding. One solution for them is finding good mentors, more-experienced people who understand that mentoring involves a lot more than wrestling through workplace issues and tasks.

At the same time, we have the virtually untapped resource of wise, veteran business and professional leaders who don't realize how much they have to offer — or how to provide it. Recently, I was meeting with a CEO who had volunteered to be part of a formal mentoring program sponsored by a university. He started with a passion to mentor others, but became so stifled by the rigid guidelines and the university's systematic approach that he felt like a miserable failure. The experience seemed so dismal, the executive had nearly decided never to attempt being a mentor again.

From the start, I could see this CEO had become discouraged, convinced that he had failed because he didn't have much to offer. But as we met, I also could see that this man was extremely talented and had a tremendous amount to give — and he really had a heart for mentoring others. He just needed some insight into how to go about it properly, an understanding of foundational principles, and the freedom to mentor someone without being confined by arbitrary structures and restrictions. Today he is actively mentoring several executives and finding greater fulfillment through these relationships than he had ever imagined possible.

A GREAT WAY TO LEAVE A LEGACY

Today, after years of enjoying the privilege of mentoring other men, I can echo the words of my first mentor, Dave. There truly is no greater joy than giving your life away to others. People matter more than things, or goals, or achievements. And the greatest satisfaction in life comes, I believe, when you give your life away to something that really matters. Many people don't realize this, but I hope that you do — or that you will by the time you have finished reading this book.

In the Introduction I referred to the film *Finding Forrester*, in which prize-winning author William Forrester has become so consumed with himself that he has virtually removed himself from society. His only contact with the real world consists of gazing out a window from his apartment onto a playground below, where young men regularly participate in pickup basketball games.

Then he meets Jamal, a young, aspiring writer who does everything but beg Forrester to mentor him. Reluctantly, Forrester agrees and, much to his surprise, it's not an unpleasant experience. As the relationship grows, Forrester — despite having extricated himself from everyday affairs — begins to get his life back. He breaks out of his hermit-like shell and discovers for himself that he is more fulfilled by giving some of himself away.

Thinking back to the man I met near the waterfall, I know that with his professional background he could have been a very effective and fulfilled mentor if he simply understood this principle. His head was into mentoring — he was convinced it was a worthwhile thing to do — but his heart was not in it. How different it might have been for him if, rather than just going through the motions, he had grasped the idea that mentoring is a function of the heart. It is not what we get out of it, but rather what we can put into it — without preconceived expectations or fixed agendas.

My desire throughout this book is not just to provide you with information. In this so-called "communications age," we already feel consumed by more information than we could ever use. I want to help in moving you to action, providing you with fundamental principles for getting started in this exciting adventure. Skills and methods are important, but to succeed in mentoring it is even more crucial that we start first with the heart.

If your purpose in reading this book is to nail down *the* method for mentoring, you won't find it here, because there is no single effective method for mentoring. We have enough methodology out there already. Effective, life-changing mentoring is a product of relationships and principles. If we master the key principles, then our methods and skills can come alive. But the first principle to master is that mentoring starts with the heart, with the understanding that living is about giving.

As we close this chapter, I have a question for you: What are *you* giving your life to? Don't respond too quickly. To help you in answering as honestly as possible, I have provided a series of self-examination questions below. Please consider each question and respond, not as you think you should, but as you truly see yourself right now.

Go ahead. Be honest. I won't tell anyone. After you have finished these questions, I'll meet you in chapter 2, where we will take a look, not at a final destination, but at the journey we call *mentoring*.

A Mentoring Self-Examination

1. Do you see yourself as self-centered? Why or why not?
2. What do you consider to be your strengths, both personally and vocationally?
3. What are some of the most significant successes and failures you have experienced in your life?
4. Who are the people who have had a positive impact on you as mentors or in other ways? What specifically did they do?
5. At this point in your life, how would you summarize the legacy you are establishing? How might being involved in mentoring enhance your legacy?

IT'S THE JOURNEY THAT COUNTS

••

PRINCIPLE #2: EFFECTIVE MENTORS SEE MENTORING AS A

PROCESS THAT REQUIRES PERSEVERANCE.

••

*W*e live in what some observers have characterized as a microwave society. Forget the old saying, "A watched pot never boils." We grow impatient having to wait just a few minutes, even seconds, for the microwave oven to beep! If you live in a big city as I do, when you get caught in the inevitable traffic jam, you wish you could be "teleported" to your destination in moments just by requesting, "Beam me up, Scotty!" as in the old *Star Trek* episodes.

We fidget during the few seconds it takes for our computers to come on, and we grit our teeth when we place a call to question a billing statement and hear the dreaded words, "Can you hold, please?" We even lose patience at fast-food restaurants, convinced that "have it your way" means having it instantaneously, without delay. I can remember when we used to wait several days for important documents to arrive via what we now term "snail mail." These days we call out to administrative assistants, asking in urgent voices, "Did that overnight package arrive yet?"

You could add countless other examples. It's not that the pace of this microwave society is necessarily wrong. I'm all in favor of speedy printers and copiers, TVs that come to life instantly at the touch of a remote, lightning-fast access to Web sites on the Internet, and consumer loans that can be approved in minutes. I can't imagine what I would do without the immediacy of my cell phone. But the fact of the matter is, some things just cannot be rushed.

If you are a parent, you know what I mean. No matter what you do, you can't get a newborn to act like a three-year-old. And three-year-olds just aren't ready to act like six-year-olds. And adolescents, even precocious ones, aren't inclined to act like adults.

The no-rush principle also is true of gardening. For instance, it takes effort and time to grow an abundant crop of ripe tomatoes. You don't just stick tomato plants in the ground, wait a minute or two, and grab ripened fruit off the vine, ready for a salad or juicy burger. It takes weeks of nurture, watchful attention, and even protective intervention if your garden is to yield tasty, bright-red tomatoes for your dinner table.

Unfortunately, when we think about mentoring, we often apply our microwave mindset and expect to reap instant results. We wrap programs, structures, agendas, and timelines around the mentoring concept as if it were some ready-to-serve meal. But if we try to develop people according to this mindset, we fail to tap into the vast, life-changing impact of mentoring — for both the mentor and the mentoring partner.

When I first started mentoring other men, my approach reflected this kind of microwave mentality — a "get results fast" attitude. I was immersed in a thriving sales career and a growing family, so time was a constant concern for me. When I sat down to begin mentoring someone, I arrived with an agenda and expected to see results — fast. I wanted a maximum return on my investment, as quickly as possible. For instance, early in my adventure into the world of mentoring, I met with a young man named Andy. He was a nice guy, very gregarious, but after a few weeks it occurred to me that I wasn't seeing the changes I had expected. Andy wasn't following through on assignments I had asked him to complete.

So one afternoon I showed up at his office, determined to end the mentoring relationship. I was convinced it was a waste of my time. Hoping to find an easy way out, I asked Andy, "Why do you want to keep meeting with me?" His answer surprised me. With a quiet, humble tone, he replied, "Because I really want to be like you." Basically, he was saying that he also wanted to experience success in business and more balance in his life, but didn't have a clue about where or how to get started. Andy had seen some things in me that he thought would be helpful, and he was expecting me to point the way.

When Andy said that, I was dumbfounded. From what I had seen, it appeared that nothing was happening, but deep inside he already was changing. It reminded me of a plant that grows from a seed. For a while, if you just watch the surface of the ground, there seems to be no activity. You could easily conclude that nothing is happening. Then one day you notice a tiny shoot of green sticking out of the soil, and before long you have an abundance of growth. Suddenly, you realize, "Man! There really was a flower in there after all."

As Andy and I concluded our meeting that day, our relationship did not come to an end. He was just beginning to bud. But he taught me — the mentor — a very important principle: Mentoring is a process that requires great perseverance. Perseverance in mentoring is a commitment to the process of mentoring no matter how long it takes. Putting it another way, it's an opportunity to take a journey with another person in traveling the uncharted path of life. Andy showed me that I needed to lighten up, let go of my goals and expectations, and focus only on how I could be most helpful to him. The question I want you to consider as you continue reading is this: *Are you willing to persevere with someone on this type of journey?*

Andy helped me to look back on my experience with my first mentor, Dave, who had a clear understanding that mentoring me would entail a process, or a journey that we would take together. I'm glad Dave didn't expect fast results from me, because our relationship would never have sustained itself that way. He stayed by me even when it appeared as if nothing were happening in my life — at least not anything positive. He never quit on me, even though there were times when I was ready to quit on myself.

If we really think about it, we understand that in many ways life is a journey. Physical, mental, emotional, and spiritual growth all take time. The same is true of our work. My career started in sales, progressed into management, and later moved to running an organization. But it didn't happen overnight. Incremental steps were necessary before I could advance to each successive stage of my career. We all have experienced this, but when it comes to working with other people, we often forget what we know from our own lives. We want results from people as rapidly as possible, despite our awareness that similar results for us may have come slowly, sometimes painfully.

Think in terms of growth, which always involves a process, whether you're referring to trees, babies, or mentoring partners. For this reason, I also like to use the term *journey* because it implies an adventure and a fair amount of uncertainty, even if you have a good notion of your intended destination. Sometimes the journey takes you to places where you never expected to go.

Carl was twenty-seven when we started meeting about seven years ago. We had met in a Bible discussion group I was leading for an unusual assortment of young men. Groups like this can be a great place to find men who have an interest in being mentored.

To be honest, my first impression of Carl was not a good one. He seemed cocky and stubborn — not exactly the qualities you seek in a teachable, receptive mentoring partner. In fact, I wasn't sure that any of the men in the group would be good mentoring prospects.

One morning, after the group had been meeting for several months, Carl approached me and stated that he wanted to start learning how to invest in people as I was doing. I agreed to meet with him, emphasizing what I tell every man at the outset of a mentoring relationship: There is no binding commitment either way. If, for whatever reason, either of us no longer wants to meet, we can quit at any time.

But I was amazed, and pleasantly surprised, when we started meeting. Carl proved to be extremely coachable and very eager to learn, not only about how to invest in others, but also concerning how to deal with various issues he was facing related to marriage, his career, his finances, and life in general.

Thankfully, by this time I had learned to cast aside any agenda and timeline for mentoring and was able to focus on Carl's needs and expectations. At first we just hung out together, spending time at a restaurant or in some other casual setting, taking the time to get to know one another better. We clicked, and a strong bond began to form as mentor and mentoring partner. Out of our unstructured times together came structure as I gained a clearer understanding of Carl's needs and as he captured a better grasp of specifics he wanted to learn and discover.

He was not married when we started meeting, but today Carl is happily married with two children, has built a successful professional career, and maintains a relatively well-balanced life. He is even doing what he initially said he wanted to do — investing in others by mentoring them, as he learned to do through our time together.

Seven years later, Carl and I still meet, but not as frequently, and now we enjoy more of a peer relationship. We talk about important issues we are working through, solicit one another's counsel, and provide mutual encouragement. Without hesitation, I can honestly say I have gained as much from this relationship as Carl has — possibly more. Not every mentoring relationship extends for that long, of course, but this is not an exception, either. If you stay with the process, even when results are not as forthcoming as desired, more often than not your perseverance will be rewarded.

MENTORING IS A DYNAMIC PROCESS

Mentoring is a dynamic process, not a static, one-size-fits-all program. It involves a journey that is active, vibrant, and ever-changing because people are complex, changing, unique individuals, not static commodities that fit neatly into a box with expected outcomes geared to strict timetables. Through my years of mentoring, I have never ceased to marvel at the endless variety of people I meet: men and women of different interests, talents, strengths, needs, and issues demanding resolution. And in every mentoring relationship I have had, no two have ever been the same.

In his book *The Fifth Discipline*, Peter Senge offers a captivating insight about teaching and learning: "Many of the best-intentioned efforts to foster new learning disciplines founder because those leading the charge forget the first rule of learning: people learn what they need to learn, not what someone else thinks they need to learn."[1] Each mentor — and mentoring partner — is different and should not be squeezed into someone else's arbitrary mold.

I've seen this often in organizations, especially in the nonprofit arena. To manage, measure, and control masses of people, mentoring programs that have very specific timelines, agendas, curricula, and so on, are put in place. In many cases the emphasis is on the program's agenda or the curriculum instead of on the person or the process. The pitfall of forcing mentoring into a box and being overly structured or restricted by schedules is that it leaves little room for new thinking or real learning. We lose sight of the possibility of helping a person reach his or her fullest potential in life. The task becomes the focus, not the individual. As a result, people are not mentored in the fullest sense.

That's why I shake my head in wonder at mentoring programs that treat individuals as if they are clones, all stamped out of the same mold. Somehow we believe that we can relate to people as if they are stagnant, inert entities.

Remember the story in the previous chapter about the first man I tried to mentor, the guy whose name I can't even remember? My primary problem there was in perceiving him as an inadaptable individual, someone who was not willing to follow my agenda and fit into my program. But he didn't want assignments; he wanted a relationship with someone he respected and could talk with and learn from concerning important issues in his life. Because I didn't see it as a dynamic process, it was a lose-lose for both of us.

People have grown weary of programs and with promises of simple solutions for complex problems. Many executives I meet with talk about spending large sums of money on programs, with outcomes that prove to be short term at best. They are tired of results that do not — and cannot — sustain themselves.

I don't mean to dismiss the value of formal mentoring and training programs. Good things can and do happen in that scenario: training for specific skills, preparation for working on a key project, or orientation to equip an individual to assume new job responsibilities. In one respect, formal mentoring programs serve much like apprenticeships, with the more experienced, practiced "experts" imparting insight to the people being mentored. This can be invaluable for the success of a business or organization of any size. But when the emphasis becomes the program, not the journey with the person, it's a poor use of invaluable time and resources.

My first formal corporate mentor as I launched my career in sales understood this. Although his official title was sales trainer, Craig understood that there was more to what I needed than product knowledge and instruction in how to close a sale. I loved the time I spent with him, because even though much of our time was focused on my job and selling skills, we could talk about any topic at all. Whether he realized it or not, he engaged me in a learning process in which I was the center of attention, not him. He saw me as a whole person with needs that extended far beyond getting someone to put a signature at the bottom of an order form. As a matter of fact, he stayed with me on the journey until I succeeded in becoming a sales trainer myself.

We can learn in both structured and nonstructured ways. Frankly, I'm a guy who is highly structured to an extreme, so inserting people into a narrow framework to achieve certain objectives fits my style very well. I feel very comfortable with defined, established structure in whatever I do. But over time I have learned that when we focus on the program, rather than seeing mentoring as a process in constant flux (because people are continually changing with various needs), we can stifle creativity and discourage learning.

Granted, a process that looks like it requires long-term commitment without guaranteed results can be a daunting thought, especially for citizens of a microwave society. But when we can accept that mentoring — formal or informal — entails a journey with another individual through life and we're willing to persevere in this journey, then we have jumped a major hurdle.

PERSEVERANCE REQUIRES PATIENCE

In a mentoring relationship, giving advice may be easy, but it's not always helpful. Someone tells you about a problem or struggle he or she is having and, drawing from your vast store of experience, you feel inclined to reply, "Here is what you need to do. . . . " Unfortunately, that kind of response creates two problems. It sets the mentor above the mentoring partner, disrupting the sense of a mutually beneficial relationship. Also, while it may provide a quick fix for the immediate situation, it doesn't help the partner to learn how to work through difficulties on his or her own. Admittedly, many times it is hard not to offer advice, because the solution seems so obvious to the mentor. Hence the need for patience — being willing to wait for growth to occur without getting frustrated. Like a farmer who endures the planting and cultivating process, waiting patiently for the harvest, we need patience to watch the mentoring partner wrestle through issues at the slow, plodding pace of a novice, without jumping in to "fix it."

In chapter 1, I told you about Don, who was the first guy I had some degree of success with in mentoring. Well, here's the rest of that story. A day came when I reverted to my old tendencies and started focusing on Don's behavior. He wasn't doing some of the things I had urged him to do, so I became frustrated with his progress — or lack of it. I wanted to see faster results so I could check him off my "to do" list and move on to the next mentoring project. My response was to put on my "sales hat" and become overbearing, trying to push him along. Understandably, he didn't appreciate this change in my attitude. Slowly, our relationship dissolved and we stopped meeting. Instead of accepting him where he was, I simply thought it better to move on.

Unfortunately, that terminated my first "successful" mentoring experience. My young friend had made some progress, just not as much as I thought he should have. Even though my criticisms were well intentioned, I turned him away because I wasn't willing to be patient. I should have been more understanding, recognizing that he was still very much "in process." In the years since, I have realized that if a mentor truly desires to give his or her life away to others, the best expectations to have are no expectations. Thankfully, I have learned from this experience. The one positive is that it has served as a valuable lesson for me about patience and not trying to force growth.

PERSEVERANCE REQUIRES PERSISTENCE

Persistence is constantly encouraging and even constructively reproving your mentoring partner on issues that take a long time to change. Sometimes this means revisiting an issue over and over again because the mentoring partner just doesn't "get it."

I'm reminded of one sharp young man I was mentoring. Ken was intelligent, athletic, very relational, and highly teachable. Despite these positive and enviable attributes, he struggled with a poor self-image and failed to appreciate his abilities. Meeting almost every week for six months, we talked about only one thing. Ken would say, "I'm just worthless," expressing his feeling that no one respected him.

Money was not a problem for him, because his family was very wealthy. In fact, the abundance of money was part of his problem. Ken didn't have a job where he could find fulfillment; he had no sense of what his niche in life might be. So, week after week we would engage in the same conversation: He would tell me how worthless he felt, and I would do my best to challenge his distorted thinking.

Believe me, a few months of the same conversation was not easy, but I perceived great potential in Ken. I knew it would just take time for him to see it, too. The most important thing was his willingness to continue meeting, showing that he was hungry and wanting to learn how to get his life steered in the right direction. We have been meeting for more than two years, and it has been a delight to see how he has grown personally and vocationally during that time. He still is not where I would like him to be someday, but through persistent encouragement and "staying power" in this journey, he will finally fulfill the incredible potential that still lies largely untapped within him.

PERSEVERANCE REQUIRES TIME

Right now, one little word might be troubling you: T-I-M-E. You might be wrestling with the notion of meeting with someone for months, and possibly years. "I don't even have time for an appointment two hours from now, let alone to commit to meet with someone week after week for who knows how long!"

If you're feeling this way, I'm not surprised. It's an honest response — and very understandable. But I would like to suggest two ideas that can free you from viewing this as some kind of burden.

First, as I mentioned before, whenever I meet with someone in a mentoring relationship, I let the partner know *there is no commitment.* Either of us can walk at any time if we don't think our time together is profitable. When you live in a microwave society, long-range planning typically doesn't extend much beyond the next weekend, so the lower the commitment level, the better. I state up front to my partners that if the time isn't meaningful, they can stop, no hard feelings. For many people, a twelve- or eighteen-month commitment seems like forever. Why add unnecessary pressure? Just agree to meet until one or the other feels it no longer serves a beneficial purpose.

Second, I *put the ball in his court.* I let the partner know that I am totally available, that I would be glad to mentor him — if he wants me to. The initiative for continuing the relationship is his. Sometimes I purposely "forget" to set up another meeting. I let it go and see if my mentoring partner will call back. If he doesn't, I don't pursue him, because the answer is clear: He has little or no interest in proceeding. Once our relationship starts to grow, however, it becomes more of a mutual pursuit because we are forming a close friendship.

This not only relieves the pressure of a long-term obligation, but also tests the sincerity of the parties involved. A mentoring relationship will survive on its own merits. If the mentoring partner is eager, coachable, and serious about learning, he or she will make it a priority to meet with the mentor. But if the partner isn't serious, perhaps having decided to seek a mentor just because it sounded like a good thing to do, it will quickly come to an end.

It's important not to downplay the fact that mentoring definitely requires time, energy, and a lot of personal investment. If it didn't, it wouldn't be worthwhile for either party. Near the close of the '90s, studies showed that the most important commodity for most people was no longer money, but time. Whether you are rich or poor, you receive twenty-four hours a day, 168 hours each week, no more and no less. The fact is, we can't actually "manage" time; all we can do is allocate it. But I have seen over and over again that if you have a passion for something, you *will* make time for it. Whether it's your marriage, your children, your job, a beloved hobby, or your favorite sports team, if you have a passion for it, you will "find" the time to devote to it. This is true of mentoring as well. Once you have discovered first-hand what it's like to invest part of yourself in someone else and have watched with amazement as you've been an instrument to help change another person's life, you *will* acquire a passion for mentoring and won't have trouble finding the time for it.

Many of the guys I meet with find themselves stretched to the maximum. They are extremely busy. Many of them are still working hard to build their careers. But if one of their kids becomes ill or another emergency arises, well-planned schedules go out the window while they attend to what is really important. If mentoring becomes one of the facets of your life that fits in the "really important" category, you won't have trouble fitting it into your schedule.

When Anne and I got married in 1980, I didn't regard our marriage as a mentoring relationship, but in a sense that is what it has been. We have been on a journey together since day one, and we have been learning and growing together all along the way. And much of what we have learned has occurred in the course of daily living. In a marriage, you can't just quit; you have to continue working at it, keeping the relationship strong and growing. While a mentoring relationship does not have the moral and legal ties of marriage, the principle is similar. You embark together on a journey, perhaps not one that will last for the rest of your lives, but one that has the potential to profoundly affect both of you.

WHEN IS IT TIME TO STOP PERSEVERING?

At this point, another question arises: How do you know when this journey, this mentor-mentoring partner relationship, should end? Even if you have a heart for mentoring — and *especially* if you have a heart for mentoring — you still have a finite amount of time at your disposal. Because there are other people who need to be mentored, is there a logical point when the relationship should end?

If you're a structured type of person, you would probably feel greatly relieved if I declared that the mentoring relationship definitely should end after a maximum number of meetings or months — or years. But there is no secret formula. People don't grow in a straight line, and the process takes longer for some than for others. But I can offer some helpful ideas.

You meet as long as the mentoring partner keeps coming back. The best partners are great learners, and if they remain teachable and coachable, you want to be there for them. You are working with emerging leaders and, hopefully, future mentors! Even when partners move to other cities or states, quality relationships can and should be maintained, if desired. Sometimes I like to periodically ask the question, "Do we still need to meet?" If not, now is as good a time as any to find out.

You only schedule one meeting at a time. If you don't schedule meetings far into the future, it reinforces the understanding that there is no long-term commitment, and both parties are free to stop at any time without feelings of obligation or guilt for not going on.

You can end before you start. Occasionally, it might become apparent that the mentoring partner, and not the mentor, has a hidden agenda. It could be that he or she wants help in finding a job or is trying to make a sale. While networking to achieve such objectives is common, that is not the purpose of mentoring. If I am meeting with someone and detect a motive other than a desire to be mentored, I end it as soon as possible. Agendas — on either side — are not acceptable.

Like-mindedness or like-heartedness between mentor and mentoring partner is essential. If we do not share the same common interest or purpose — to grow and to learn together — effective mentoring cannot take place.

Mentors choose their partners, not vice versa. The mentor exercises the choice of whether to mentor someone, because time and energy are limited. It's okay to say no, for whatever reason. One time a woman said to a friend of Anne's, "God told me that you were supposed to mentor me." Graciously, Anne's friend replied, "God hasn't shown me that yet, but I'll let you know if He does."

Meetings should become less frequent over time. Even in long-term mentoring, you don't continue to meet at the same frequency. Early on, important ongoing issues may call for getting together every week, possibly more often than that. But as the mentoring partner's life begins to change, reducing dependence upon the mentor, the need to meet as often diminishes.

Look at it this way: In some respects, mentoring is similar to a parent-child relationship. Do we get rid of our children when they make a mess? No, we stick with the process. What about when they are grown? We still don't sever ties with them, but the time we spend with them diminishes along with their dependence on us. Yet we remain available to them whenever they need us. This has been the case as well for men I have mentored, such as Carl and Ken.

One difference between mentoring and parenting may be in the area of expectations. With our children we have certain expectations: to see that they receive an education; to teach them to behave in certain ways; to introduce them to sports, music, and other beneficial avocations; to teach them the values of work and responsibility; and so on. But in mentoring, it's important to keep our expectations low and simply to be available to help the partners pursue their own objectives. Our only expectation should be for their personal growth, but even then we can't control how they grow. Mentors can inspire, encourage, raise questions, and facilitate learning, but they cannot change people. Ultimately, their motivation has to come from within.

I hope by now I have convinced you that mentoring truly is a journey that requires perseverance with another person, but that still leaves us with a dilemma. One of the by-products of a microwave society is relationships that are only skin deep and interactions that don't go much beyond "Hi. How are you?" and "Fine. How are you?" This won't get you very far in mentoring. If you're going on a journey with someone, wouldn't it be helpful to get to know that person in more than a superficial way?

To effectively mentor people, you need to know how to get into their world, but as you can imagine, many times that is not as easy as it sounds. So how do you get into their world? Meet me in chapter 3 and we'll discuss that question.

But first, while this chapter is fresh on your mind, I would like to stir your thinking with several other questions.

Thoughts About the Journey

1. Have you seen your life as a journey? Why or why not? What kind of journey has it been?

2. Think of a time when someone exhibited one or more of the following in their relationship with you: perseverance, patience, and persistence. What did that mean for you?

3. Would you describe yourself as highly structured, someone who functions best with well-defined guidelines and objectives? Why or why not? How does this affect how you view mentoring?

4. How important to you is it to be able to get fast results from what you do? What bearing might this have on your effectiveness as a mentor or mentoring partner?

CHAPTER 3

INTO THEIR WORLD—THROUGH YOURS

· ·

PRINCIPLE #3: EFFECTIVE MENTORS OPEN THEIR WORLD
TO THEIR MENTORING PARTNERS.

· ·

A friend recently told me about visiting his physician's office for treatment of a minor ailment. The problem was more of an annoyance than anything, but as he described his symptoms, the doctor held himself aloof and looked at his patient with a puzzled expression.

"I don't like going to doctors anyway," my friend admitted. "All I wanted to do was explain what the problem was, have my physician nod reassuringly, tell me he understood what I was talking about, and then prescribe something to make the symptoms go away.

"But that puzzled look bothered me. Suddenly, I felt as if my 'minor ailment' might be some dreaded, rare disease that until that moment had never been encountered by medical science. *Please, Doc, I began thinking to myself. Tell me that this is really a common problem that can be treated very easily!*"

As it turned out, my friend's ailment did have a simple remedy. But can you imagine how it felt to go to the "expert" and receive little or no empathy or understanding? Unfortunately, this is the experience of many men and women as they enter into mentoring relationships. They want help from people they regard as experts in dealing with a variety of issues, but they also want reassurance that they are not alone, that the rocky road they are traveling has already been successfully negotiated by others.

Remember Kyle in the Introduction? He had been looking for a vibrant, two-way relationship, but instead, every time he met with his first mentor he felt he was being observed through a microscope. Kyle would try to open up, pouring out his heart, but his mentor would just sit and listen dispassionately, offering little in response. Can you blame Kyle for feeling frustrated after a while? There's not much give-and-take when you're the only one doing the giving.

Once you recognize that to effectively mentor someone you must deal with the whole person — both the personal and the professional life, not an isolated fragment of his or her life — the challenge is to get to know that "whole person." Occasionally, you may come across an open-book type like Kyle, but most individuals are not as eager to submit their innermost being to close scrutiny. To get someone to open up, you could try a straightforward approach, something like, "Okay, tell me all about yourself. Tell me your hurts, your needs, your deepest passions and ambitions. Give me the whole story." Yes, you *could* do that, but it usually doesn't work. As we said in the previous chapter, our microwave society has fostered superficial relationships. We're not accustomed to going below the surface with other people, especially those who are virtually strangers.

So how *do* you get into their lives, learning what their struggles and challenges are, their needs, passions, and ambitions? It's simple, really, and effective mentors will do this: *You open your own world.* In other words, to get into the mentoring partner's world, we have to let them into our world. And to open our world to those we mentor, we must first learn to meet them where they are, not where we think they're supposed to be.

THE BIG DADDY SYNDROME

Barry Spencer is a twenty-something who has become a valuable member of our Leader's Legacy team. Years ago, he moved from Detroit, Michigan, to Atlanta in pursuit of a career dream, and I started to mentor him a few weeks later. Barry is very outgoing, but even so, he was very hesitant initially to share freely. Most older adults, he had discovered, didn't seem to care much about his life. They only wanted to give him advice to "fix" the problem. But by the end of our first meeting, he began inviting me into his world, even though I'm more than twenty years older.

He said I made him feel so safe because he knew that I really cared about him. How? I met him right where he was. I related to him at his level. Most of the time we talked about him and what was going on in his life. There were times when I would share snapshots of my own life, but my desire was simply to reflect on instances when my personal experiences seemed to parallel his. When the mentor demonstrates an ability to relate to what the mentoring partner is going through, that creates a safe environment for openness and honesty.

The key, I believe, is the mentor's willingness to "come down from the mountain" — to leave the lofty perch of success and authority — and simply to walk alongside the mentoring partner. This is a way of showing that you don't feel "above" the other person; you are just further along in the process. As Barry explained to me, "Dave, guys my age have a general sense of where we want to go in life, but to get there we know it's an uphill battle with a lot of obstacles in the way. Although we will never be rid of obstacles, many of these look like mountains. A mentor can help us turn a lot of these mountains into molehills. Instead of shouting down to us, 'Hurry up!' mentors need to come back and walk with us."

Some time ago I came across the following poem on the Internet:

> Don't walk behind me, I will not lead;
> Don't walk in front of me, I will not follow;
> Just walk beside me and be my friend.

These words sum up clearly and concisely the desires and expectations of mentoring partners and prospective partners today. Partners want someone they can respect, who is more knowledgeable and experienced, yet who does not "lord it over" them, making them feel more insecure than they already do.

The last line of the poem, "Just walk beside me and be my friend," reminds me of when I was a boy and would spend leisurely summer days hanging out with my friends. It's amazing the openness we had toward one another, the secrets we confided with each other, the joys we shared together. In mentoring, I think a dimension of this kind of candor is necessary.

Over the years I have seen many mentoring relationships fail because the mentor puts himself or herself above the mentoring partner. Even the companion terms *mentor* and *mentee* or *mentoree* reek of one-upmanship. This is why I prefer the term *mentoring partner*. It conveys equality, more of a peer relationship.

I'm grateful that my mentors never treated me like a lower-class "mentee." My dear friend Mark Pollard, founder of the National

Common Ground Coalition, a not-for-profit organization that mentors men in the inner cities, calls this the Big Daddy syndrome. He says, "It's an attitude of, 'I don't need you. You need me.' This is arrogance. We are committed to it scientifically, but we don't love the guy."

Research on mentoring among professionals of color has found that those who "plateaued in management received mentoring that was basically instructional; it helped them develop better skills. Minority executives, by contrast, enjoyed closer, fuller developmental relationships with their mentors. This was particularly true in people's early careers, when they needed to build confidence, credibility, and competence. That is, purely instructional mentoring was not sufficient; protégés needed to feel connected to their mentors."[1]

This need, as we have already noted, is not restricted to people of color. There must be a connectedness between mentors and mentoring partners regardless of race, ethnic background, or gender.

Sometimes the fact that people are not where we think they should be can blind us to their need for mentoring in the first place. A while back I met with Harry, a recent MBA grad who was feeling very disillusioned. He had learned about a local businessmen's organization through the Internet, one that I had been involved with at one time, so I suggested that he check it out. He and a friend had eagerly showed up for the subsequent morning meeting, anticipating the opportunity to start gleaning from the experience of other men in this group.

When he arrived, Harry felt even more fired up. He saw a number of men who obviously were very successful and seasoned, so he decided that if one of them offered an invitation to lunch, he and the friend would quickly accept. To their disappointment, they were virtually ignored. Other than a casual hello, the young men were treated as if they didn't exist. "No way will I ever go back there," Harry declared.

Ironically, during my association with this group, I had often heard some of the men talking about their desire to mentor others. They had a golden opportunity right in front of them but failed to take advantage of it. They would not come down to Harry's level and accept these young businessmen where they were instead of where they were "supposed" to be.

Now and then I have encountered mentors who exalt themselves. This is unfortunate because this kind of approach destroys the partnering quality and the potential of the relationship. Just as we elect our president and other government officials to serve the people, mentors need to embrace the role of *serving and exalting their mentoring partners*. We should relate to them as equals, cultivating a servant leadership heart that values the mentoring partner's interests more than our own. The Bible offers great insight in this regard. Jesus said, "The one who is greatest among you must become like the youngest, and the leader like the servant" (Luke 22:26, NASB).

MENTORING WITH EMOTIONAL INTELLIGENCE

Now that we have seen the wisdom of "coming down from the mountain," let's consider how to get into the mentoring partner's world. As we said earlier, the most effective way to do this is by letting the partner into our world. Studies in leadership today repeatedly show that the most effective leaders have a high degree of emotional intelligence (ability to relate to people). They are authentic. They reveal their weaknesses. They are down-to-earth, genuine people who are approachable, not distant and emotionally detached.

In his book *Executive EQ: Emotional Intelligence in Leadership and Organizations*, Robert K. Cooper makes this powerful observation:

"Unless I can come to know what is real about you — something of your life story, what you care about and stand for, what you feel as well as what you know — you do not actually exist for me beyond your name, job title, and appearance. I cannot know you or have a genuine dialogue, which, by definition, sets for us as its implicit goal *shared meaning.*"[2]

Later in the book, Cooper writes, "When we get inspired and motivated, it is by real people, the ones with a good head on their shoulders, of course, but always with a heart. No one expects a leader to be perfect — only genuine and honest." Such people possess, he points out, "the courage to find themselves, to tell the truth about who they are, the mistakes they have made, the dreams they hold, and what they're most concerned about, and excited about, in growing the business or in growing their life. This is the bedrock for open dialogue and trust."[3]

This is what young people want in a mentor — someone who is real, who can relate with the joys, struggles, and everyday issues they encounter. Because mentoring is a two-way learning and growing process, when we show that we are real, it becomes safer for our partners to be real with us.

So how do I let my mentoring partner into my world? The most significant way is to let them know about my difficulties and struggles, especially as they relate to what they are going through. I usually tell them up front, "Hey man, I'm going to be open about my life, so you can be open about yours."

Of course, it helped me greatly to hear my mentor openly share about his own weaknesses and failures, and as I have mentored others it has been amazing how my willingness to talk about my struggles and difficulties has freed them to open the door to their own lives.

When George and I met for the first time, he had just lost his job. Our conversation stayed at a very superficial level, and I suspected it was because George was too embarrassed to talk about the humility and uncertainty of suddenly being without work. I knew a lot of questions were probably running through his mind: How he was going to support his wife and kids? What would happen if he couldn't find another job soon? Would they lose their house?

Hoping to move our conversation to a deeper, more meaningful level, I admitted, "George, I can't relate to not having a job. That's never happened to me, but I really can relate to the kind of pain you're experiencing, the sense of humiliation of not knowing whether you're going to be able to pay the bills and put food on the table."

I explained to George about going through two years of almost unbearable financial difficulty after I got out of college. With my credit card maxed out, combined with car loans and student loans, there was a time when I didn't know how I would survive. As George realized that I could relate to what he was going through, I saw a glimmer of hope on his face. Suddenly, he didn't feel alone.

Seeing me as a comrade in pain, he began pouring out his heart about how devastating it felt to lose his job and how he also had overextended himself financially. He didn't expect me to solve his problems, but knowing I had "gone before him," George knew I could provide experienced insight as he traveled down the same path. From that moment, our mentoring relationship took off. It required some time and a lot of hard work and determination, but today George is debt free except for his mortgage and a small car loan. The lost job? In retrospect he sees it as a blessing disguised as a bombshell. It enabled him to take stock of his life's work, leading him to make a major career shift, and now he is doing work he truly loves.

I'm afraid that too often when we get into mentoring relation-ships we shy away from exposing our weaknesses or vulnerabilities, feeling we need to present a bold, strong front. But admitting where we struggle doesn't diminish our effectiveness; it enhances it. When we offer examples of our own struggles, our mentoring partners know we are talking from experience, not hypothetically. They don't want just success stories; they want to know how we got to where we are — and part of that process was dealing with the inevitable adver-sities of life and work. Our candor greatly enhances our credibility and their trust in us.

Perhaps this talk about "being real" has made you feel somewhat uncomfortable. If so, maybe it's because you were taught not to share openly about your life, or because by nature you tend to be private about personal matters. You may even be wondering something like, "Just how *open* am I supposed to be?"

I really cannot answer that for you because it depends on your comfort level in unfolding aspects of your private life to others. Personally, I don't have a problem in being open with other people. In fact, I often tell the men I am mentoring that they can ask me any-thing because I have nothing to hide. I'm learning, too. Of course, we also understand from the outset that we must observe mutual confi-dentiality: I won't tell anyone their secrets and I expect them to guard any confidences I share with them as well. Such openness doesn't happen on the first meeting. Trust takes time to develop, so you take it slowly, but as you gradually learn that you can talk about personal matters without the information becoming tomorrow's headlines, openness becomes easier.

In this discussion of openness, it might be helpful to mention that there is a difference between transparency and vulnerability. In their excellent book, *The Ascent of a Leader,* Bill Thrall, Bruce McNicol, and Ken McElrath comment, "Vulnerability does not mean transparency. Transparency is simply disclosing yourself to others at times and in ways you choose. Although transparency is a good start, in vulnerability you deliberately place yourself under others' influence, submitting yourself to others' strengths. . . . You choose to let others know you, to have access to your life, to teach you, and to influence you."[4] That may sound more like the role of the mentoring partner, but if we truly consider mentoring to be a mutually beneficial relationship, then vulnerability as well as transparency will enable it to grow deeper.

Sometimes a mentoring partner may choose to confide a reality from his or her life that will catch us off guard, but that should not negatively affect our attitude toward the individual. As mentors, we may have a sense of where we would like our mentoring partners to be eventually in their personal growth and development, but in most cases they are not there yet — and that's okay. If they were already there, they wouldn't need us.

Frankly, whenever I meet with another man, nothing surprises me anymore. That's partly because over the years I have probably encountered just about any situation that might crop up in a mentoring relationship, but also because I'm honest enough to recognize that I have had to work through a lot of my own struggles.

This might be a good place to address a topic we hear a lot about these days, particularly in the business world: accountability. While I agree that accountability needs to be a significant ingredient in a mentoring relationship, it should look much different from accountability as it is typically defined in a work setting.

More often than not, workplace accountability involves many "to do's," which puts the focus on observable behavior and performance.

If individuals fail to make acceptable progress toward their established goals, their "accountability partners" have permission to offer criticism, perhaps even ridicule. Verbally, they get shot at. While often unintended, an atmosphere of competition results in which members strive to see how much they can accomplish.

This type of accountability is far from what mentoring partners need. It doesn't help to beat up on someone who is struggling and falls short of his or her own accountability objectives. As someone once told me, accountability is about helping people to win — supporting them in the pursuit of their own goals — not about checking up on them and making sure they know it when they fail.

If the mentoring partner wishes to set an agenda — for instance by asking to be held accountable in a certain area — that is fine. It is his or her choice. But even so, as mentors we need to remain flexible, because that agenda may change — or even be discarded — at the discretion of the mentoring partner. Remember, we are here for them; they are not here for us.

SOME PRACTICAL, HELPFUL SUGGESTIONS

Because a key to getting into your mentoring partner's world is offering access to your own world, there are some very practical and helpful hints that I would like to suggest.

Harness the power of storytelling. Telling stories from our own lives is one of the best ways to show that we can relate to what the mentoring partner is going through. Sharing personal experiences shows that when we say, "I understand," we really do — at least to some degree. Even if we can't relate to a particular need or problem he or she is facing, we can communicate principles through stories, creating verbal pictures on which we can hang important concepts. Jesus was a master at this. He would tell parables — brief stories — to illustrate the principles he wanted to convey to his audiences, using scenarios that were meaningful and relevant for them.

"How Storytelling Builds Next-Generation Leaders," an article published in the Summer 2002 MIT *Sloan Management Review*, tells how, through the centuries, "storytelling has emerged as the preferred approach for teaching leadership effectiveness in many companies today."[5]

Never mentor from behind a desk. Desks create barriers and promote a sense of formality. In fact, I rarely use an office at all for mentoring. I prefer to meet in an informal and neutral setting, such as a coffee shop or restaurant. There is something about having a meal together that breaks down walls.

Often Anne and I will invite one of the men that I'm mentoring and his wife (if he has one) to come over for a meal and just hang out with our family. He gets to see me as I am, in my "natural habitat," not in some contrived, artificial business setting. Once they see us in our home, they discover that we're real, that we don't exist on some kind of pedestal. I want them to know we're just ordinary and very imperfect people, just as they are. They get to know our kids — discovering we're just plain folks — and the kids learn as well, observing firsthand our commitment to giving our lives to others.

When we open our home, mentoring partners usually let us into their "natural habitat" as well.

Listen with your heart, not just your head. There is a difference between hearing and listening. Hearing is the physical sensation of sound waves striking the eardrum, with those sounds then being interpreted by the brain. But in the act of listening, you attend to the meaning as well as to the words that are spoken. Too often we listen halfheartedly, merely waiting for the other person to pause or take a breath so we can jump into the conversation and interject our own ideas.

This proved especially true for my friend Paul, who was being mentored by Mike, a guy I had mentored. Shortly after Paul's dad died he shared with me the "story of the mop." On the day of his dad's funeral, Paul went to the church early to check on final preparations. Because the minister was already there, Paul thought it would be a good opportunity to talk with him about how the church seemed like a refuge of peace and comfort at such a dark hour.

Recalling that morning, Paul told me, "The minister listened quietly to all of this as we stood alone in the large hall. Then there was a pause. As I was about to continue, he suddenly glanced across the hall and remarked in a distracted whisper, as if thinking out loud, 'I've got to run a mop over that floor!' I stopped dead in my tracks, my disclosure aborted, the start of a friendship short-circuited. I was shocked at the unexpected shift in conversation, then felt embarrassed and foolish when I realized I had been detaining him from things he needed to do. That incident taught me a lot because I realized with painful clarity in that critical moment that we all focus on the unimportant so much of the time that we make ourselves unavailable."

Ask the right questions. This may take some practice if you're not already accustomed to it. When I was in sales I learned to ask questions that would help me to enter the world of the person I was talking with. I had a line of medical products to sell, but it was important for me to learn the needs of the person I was calling on — what problems he or she was wrestling with and how I might be able to help. As a mentor, your "product" is wisdom, experience, and expertise. But it's not about showing how much you know or how smart you are. It's about discerning the needs and concerns of the mentoring partner and discovering what kind of help you can provide.

Avoid quick fixes. Even if you can relate to your mentoring partner's particular struggle, steer clear of giving ready-made solutions. Too often, quick fixes are easily undone. They can be like putting a drop or two of solder on a metal joint; it may hold for a little while, but not for long. For years, how-to books have topped the best-seller charts, promising success in a specific endeavor in just a few easy steps. But overall, we have grown tired of quick fixes because most of the time they don't work. People are complex and so are their problems. We can offer insights and helpful suggestions, but the best assistance we can provide is simply to show sincere concern, point the way for them to discover their own solutions, and then continue on with them along their journey.

If you can't relate to your mentoring partner's struggle, just hang out. When I learned about Paul's father passing away, I could relate to what he was going through because I had lost my dad, too. But if he had been talking to me about the death of a child or going through a divorce, I could not have related to that because I have never personally experienced either situation. In circumstances like that, I have found it is best just to keep quiet and hang out with my mentoring partners. I remember when my dad died, sentiments like "I know how you feel" and "trust that it's all for the best" were well intended, but what meant the most to me were the friends who simply came by, hugged me, showed me they cared, and were available if I needed them.

Don't teach above where you are living. Try to avoid talking theoretically as you mentor someone. Instead, it's important to focus on principles you have found to work in real life, ones that are practical and relevant to the issue at hand. As a friend of mine quips, "I used to be an expert on how to raise teenagers — until I had some of my own." Don't try to bluff your way when you feel out of touch with situations others are facing. You can always admit you don't know, but promise you will try to find someone else who can relate and might be able to help. There is no shame in not understanding or not having all the answers. Admitting this, in fact, only enhances your credibility. You can't be more honest than when you tell someone, "I really don't know."

THREE WAYS MENTORS CAN HELP

Since the early 1990s, much of my emphasis in mentoring has been with young people whom we classify as Generation X — or Gen-Xers — those born between the years of 1965 and 1980. When I have heard men and women of this generation express their strong desire for mentors, I have asked, "Mentoring for what?" Their answers tend to fall in this order:

To help me with my passion.
To help me with my pain.
To help me with my priorities.

Although these are some of the issues young adults in the workplace are struggling with today, they are equally valid for older adults. To be effective in mentoring people, we need to be willing to offer assistance in each of these areas, regardless of the partner's age and experience.

Living in a world of brokenness and turmoil is cause enough for conflict, but another factor is that men and women often find themselves in working roles that fail to utilize their gifts and innate abilities in ways that produce great fulfillment. Too often these people lack a clear understanding of their own strengths and of the passions stirring inside them that could make them leap out of bed each morning, excited about tackling another day in their workplace. We will take a look at this reality in the next chapter. But first, I'd like you to consider the following questions.

Thoughts on "Getting into Their World"

1. How important is it for you to have someone to turn to who will listen and, hopefully, understand a particular challenge you are facing? Can you give an example?

2. How do you feel about getting into a mentoring partner's life by letting him or her get a glimpse of your own? Do you have any problem with the thought of being transparent — even vulnerable — with someone you are mentoring?

3. What was your reaction to the poem on page 64, "Don't walk behind me . . . "?

4. Being perfectly honest, how good are you at accepting people where they are, rather than where you think they should be?

ADDRESSING THE DESIRES OF THE HEART

• •

PRINCIPLE #4: EFFECTIVE MENTORS HELP

MENTORING PARTNERS ALIGN PASSION AND WORK.

• •

couple of years ago, a man I had been mentoring introduced me to his friend Skip, who was in his early twenties. Skip was the kind of guy who stood out — his presence, the stylish way he dressed, his infectious smile. He was one of the most relational, caring individuals I had ever met, a person who could be counted on whenever someone needed help, and he seemed without a worry in the world.

As we all know, however, appearances often deceive. As we got better acquainted through a mentoring relationship, I learned that this highly talented, charismatic young man was enduring tremendous stress. The more we talked, the more evident it became that, in terms of a career, Skip was in the wrong place. He was in sales, and while he consistently exceeded his quotas, he hated his job. He had absolutely no passion for sales and dreaded having to go to work each morning.

As outgoing as he was, you would have thought being a sales executive was the perfect job for Skip. That was how he got into sales in the first place. In college, he was so people-oriented that friends often said he should go into sales — so that's what he did. It's amazing the way well-meaning people can shape our careers, and not always for the best.

As Skip talked to me about his work, there was no hiding how much he detested what he did. It became clear that while he truly loved working with people, he yearned for a vocation that also would enable him to utilize his tremendous creative abilities.

Another man I mentored, Tim, was wrestling with similar issues. His career choice, like Skip's, had been influenced by other people. In college, Tim had told one of his professors that he wanted to start his own business one day but did not know what kind of company to start. The professor suggested that he should start an accounting firm. So Tim got an accounting degree, earned his CPA, and became a partner in a new accounting firm. After a few years, he started his own firm. When we met, Tim had sold his thriving practice to take on the new challenge of becoming the chief financial officer of a high-tech startup company, but was unmistakably miserable.

The problem wasn't money or competence, because Tim was earning a healthy income and was good in his role. For him, the question was passion. Despite his years in the field, he never had a strong interest in accounting and financial oversight. He yearned to work with people, being involved with other individuals in formulating the overall strategic direction of the company. He also loved selling. However, because of the administrative demands, Tim felt he was just a "number cruncher." This inner conflict caused him tremendous tension: It's extremely difficult to turn your back on a successful and lucrative enterprise, yet how do you continue doing work that leaves you empty at the end of the day?

When I asked Skip and Tim about their levels of productivity, both admitted they probably were functioning at less than 50 percent of their potential. Sadly, these men seem to be more the rule than the exception. Douglas McGregor notes, "Many managers would agree that the effectiveness of their organizations would be at least doubled if they could discover how to tap the unrealized potential present in their human resources."[1]

I can't count the times I have heard managers say, "People are our greatest asset," or something to that effect. They agree that getting the right person into the right job is one of their greatest challenges, and because they often fail, millions of dollars are squandered in inefficiency and diminished productivity. As management guru Peter Drucker is quoted in *Thoughts on Leadership,* "Most managers know perfectly well that of all the resources, people are the least utilized and that little of the human potential of an organization is tapped and put to work."[2]

Companies can unwittingly create cultures that hinder employee learning and growth, but the issue is much deeper than productivity and profitability. It's a matter of stewardship — for the workers and their employers. Many people today are profoundly dissatisfied with the work they do and sense they are failing to realize their potential, but find themselves without a solution. From what I have observed in mentoring, which is confirmed in a number of articles I have read, it seems evident that for many Americans in management, their need to find a deep sense of meaning and fulfillment on the job is greater than their desire for more money or more time off.

Sometimes frustration escalates to such a level that people take drastic measures to find relief. Not long ago I met a man who took a more than 50-percent cut in pay, leaving a key role in senior management, to move into a career field that could provide more personal gratification. Such extreme measures are not always warranted, but without question, our work and how we feel about it is crucial to how we regard ourselves and life in general.

One response to this might be, "Just deal with it" or "Suck it up. At least you have a job." But consider the cost in human capital of having gifted, high-caliber employees who suffer in mismatched careers. It's not only a waste of talent, but also a cause of unnecessary stress, dissatisfaction, and reduced confidence.

"CAREER"—A MOST PRESSING ISSUE

Regardless of age, most people look to their work to provide esteem, significance, and accomplishment. We each have an innate need to work. In mentoring young people, however, I have discovered that career is an even bigger issue for them because they are just starting out. Vocationally, they begin with a clean slate, and sometimes uncertainty about what they really are designed to do leads to a parade of trials — and errors. They want to know how to get established in their life's vocation. But it's more than finding a job that provides a sufficient level of financial compensation; they also want to do something that gives them a sense of meaning and fulfillment.

What we're talking about is something I like to call *passion*, which one dictionary defines as "strong feeling, either sustained or passing, for or about something or somebody." Another says passion is "a strong or extravagant fondness, enthusiasm, or desire for anything." In his excellent and insightful book *True Colors*, psychologist Roger Birkman prefers the term *interest*. He states, "Your interests are *you*. In many ways they determine how well you live, how satisfied and fulfilled you are, and how you measure your self-worth. . . . A strong interest has the status of a *need*, and the person should actively seek an outlet for this interest — at work, at home, or during leisure hours." Then he adds, "If you don't take the initiative in doing the things that are most important to you, years can pass without your knowing the satisfaction of being who you really are."[3]

As Birkman notes, it may not always be possible to pursue one's interests, or passions, in the work environment. Too often, passion and vocation are like separate tracks that never intersect. Many people I have encountered are "stuck," feeling committed to careers that don't fulfill but do provide the financial resources to pay bills and sustain their chosen lifestyles. To leave their jobs to take vocational paths that lead to personal fulfillment might also lead to poverty, or at least to a dramatic drop in income.

This poses a real dilemma because being stuck in a joyless job can cause unrelenting inner turmoil. You're not happy in what you are doing, but even if you get a picture of what you would really love to do, knowing you couldn't make it financially can make you feel like someone dying of thirst with a glass of water mere inches out of reach. So close, and yet so far.

One alternative would be to accept as fact that your job will always fit in the category of "necessary evil" and, as Birkman suggests, pursue your passion at home or during your leisure hours. However, considering the many waking hours we spend on the job, wouldn't it be preferable to find a job you feel passionate about and receive the financial return you need at the same time? Sure, but how do you make the shift? How can you leave a job that brings you no joy and find one that makes you eagerly await the start of a new day — while remaining financially viable?

First of all, it is important for mentors and mentoring partners to understand that just because someone is good at what they are doing vocationally, that does not mean it fulfills their passion. In their book *The Soul at Work*, Roger Lewin and Birute Regine state, "Deep work means developing a caring and connected relationship to yourself in terms of your work, that is, to reflect on what you are doing and why you are doing it. . . . When we connect to our passion, then work becomes love."[4]

There can be a vast difference between performance and passion. Remember Skip and Tim. Both were performing their jobs exceedingly well, but still felt miserable and desperately unfulfilled. Can you imagine what their productivity would have been like if they had loved what they were doing? What a win-win situation that would have been, both for them and for their organizations!

Many factors can collaborate to convince people to remain in jobs that set their stomachs churning when the weekend ends and the workweek resumes. People in their early thirties, for example — even if they realize they are poorly placed in a career — often feel "stuck" when they remember they have families to support and other financial obligations. At the other end of the spectrum, people in their late forties, fifties, and even sixties may look back over their decades in the workplace with regret, thinking "if only . . . ," but concluding it's too late to pursue their passions. It's my hope that as you read on, you will recognize that one need not feel either "stuck" or "too late" to make a shift that could transform a nightmare career into a dream opportunity.

As we have seen, in this journey we call mentoring, the effective mentor must succeed in getting into the mentoring partner's world. What better place to start than by mutually exploring those inner passions that beg for expression and fulfillment through work?

PERSONAL PASSIONS KNOW NO AGE LIMIT

Young people want to do work that excites them, something they enjoy and find meaningful. For more mature individuals increasingly aware of their own mortality, the desire becomes to invest their remaining time on earth in work that carries significance, something that will leave a positive legacy.

Some months ago, I was providing executive coaching for a young woman who had left a career that she thoroughly loved, but it required long hours and extensive travel. She resigned because she wanted to devote more time to her family, but since then had suffered through several unpleasant experiences in sales. Because of my own sales background, I asked why she had gotten into that line of work. Patty explained that in addition to counsel she had received from friends, she liked the idea of not having to travel out of town. However, when I asked why she had changed jobs so much, she admitted that when it came to making the necessary cold calls, "it stresses me out so much, I can't take it."

The longer we talked, the more evident it became that she was ill-suited for the demands and uncertainties of sales. Her effervescent, people-oriented nature seemed a better fit for a job in human resources or marketing. Patty looked at me with amazement, declaring, "Those are things I love to do!" She broke into tears, relieved to hear someone tell her it was okay to admit that her friends' advice had been wrong. Before long, she obtained a job in a large organization that suited her needs — and passion — very well.

I also think of Trent, an executive in his early fifties who already had attained his business goals years earlier. Money was not a concern for him, and he had grown tired of new and greater achievements.

The pressing issue on his mind was the realization that his fruitful years were ebbing away. As we met one afternoon, he commented wistfully, "You know, I may have only twenty more years to live. Maybe less than that, but I don't have anything to show for it."

Trent was acutely aware that up to this point in his life, all that he had accomplished only amounted to what the Bible calls "wood, hay, and stubble." You don't establish a legacy with "stuff," and he was seriously wondering what kind of legacy he would leave behind. From our earlier discussions, I knew he had a tremendous passion for helping people, but due to his lofty position in business, he never was able to do that in a direct, personal way.

His frustration showed sharply in his eyes, so I posed a question: "How would you like to mentor young people who would look to you for help in finding answers to the important questions in their lives?"

Trent's gaze instantly sharpened. With a sweep of his arm, pointing to all the symbols in his office of his company's success, he replied, "I would give up all of this if I could do that!"

That is why I prefer the term *passion* over *interest*. It conveys the deep emotion — the inner drive or the need to become the person you really are — that could lead to sacrificing those things our society insists should serve as the standard for measuring success.

MENTORING CAN MAKE ALL THE DIFFERENCE

In the first chapter I told how my mentor, Dave, played such an instrumental role in my early adult years. He took me to the point where I was prepared to work with others. Vocationally, however, I needed someone else to take me further along in the journey. Dave got me on my feet, but it would take another person — a second mentor — to get me running.

In 1993, Jim Petersen and I were both working with nonprofit organizations and collaborating on a cutting-edge video project in Colorado Springs, Colorado. As I watched Jim, I could see he had professional experience and insight that could help me as I pursued the vision for my career some years down the road. I sensed a need to be stretched, challenged to go far beyond what I was doing at the time.

What had intrigued me about him initially was the support he had given me during a planning session we had for the film. The project had been my idea originally, but other leaders of my organization didn't seem to care much about what I thought. During a preliminary meeting, I made a suggestion that I felt strongly about, but just about everyone around the table dismissed it. Jim hadn't said anything, so finally someone turned to him and asked, "Jim, what do you think?" Quietly, but authoritatively, he replied, "Dave's right." It blew me away to think that such a highly respected leader would support me.

One day I approached Jim and asked if he could spare a couple of hours to meet with me the next time I was in his city. I knew he did a lot of travel internationally and kept a full schedule, so I was almost afraid to request that he give me even an hour. But I wanted to meet with him so badly, I was willing to make a special trip to Colorado if necessary.

Looking at our calendars together, Jim selected a date and suggested, "Why don't we spend the day together?" Wow. I was amazed such a busy man would spend that much time with me.

As we met, I told him about my professional struggles, that I felt stifled in my company and needed some guidance on how I might be able to bring about some changes that I felt were needed. Jim had a lot of experience in working through organizational change, so I was eager to learn from him.

From the start, it was obvious that we connected well. But he never approached our relationship from a perspective of dispensing his wisdom and experience. In fact, as we talked I could see that Jim was learning as well. We engaged in free-flowing dialogue, evaluating situations and possible solutions, and we both found some "aha's" in the process.

After that first meeting, I returned home and took about two days to process all that we had discussed. Jim had really challenged my thinking, without giving any pat answers. He had enabled me to gain a greater awareness and understanding of what I needed to focus on, assigning an order of priority for steps in the process rather than trying to address everything at once.

What a difference the times with Jim made for me. Previously, I had felt totally alone in my struggles, but now I had someone who clearly was willing to walk with me through them without being judgmental or condescending. There were days when my frustration level was so high I felt like bailing out, but he encouraged me to hang on, to gain all the experience I could, and to wait for the right time before moving to something new. I'm so thankful he was there to offer a voice of restraint. Otherwise, I might have made a foolish career decision and also would have missed out on much of what I learned during my remaining years with my company.

It has been nearly ten years since Jim and I met for the first time, but we still see each other about four times a year and frequently talk by phone whenever the need arises. I find myself just as eager to discover what he has to say as when we first began to meet, and I have found Jim to be an eager learner as well. When we began getting together, I felt like a novice sitting at the feet of the master, but he makes me feel more like a fellow worker, a mentoring peer whose contributions to his life are highly valued. Often as we talk, he takes notes, giving me the amazing feeling that I have something to offer to him, that I can add something to his life.

While Jim has mentored me primarily in the areas of leadership and vocation, our relationship has grown through the years so that I can express myself openly and honestly about any subject, no matter how personal.

Most recently, Jim's greatest contribution to my life was helping me to clarify my calling, that is, what I understand to be my life's work. Since 1983, I had nurtured a passion to develop people, to help them to become true leaders. I had envisioned starting an organization that would concentrate on developing the whole person — mind, body, emotions, and spirit. My mentor had already been doing this to a great extent, and I wanted to take this passion even further. For a long time I had kept my ideas to myself, worried that no one would understand, even Jim. But finally I had to get it off my chest, and I knew Jim was the one to tell.

"I'LL BE THERE FOR YOU ALONG THE WAY"

When I started to explain this vision to him, I half expected Jim to say, "No, that's a crazy idea. Just keep doing what you're doing." But he didn't. As he listened, Jim grew as excited as I was. We talked about different aspects of my idea, but in essence he was simply saying, "Go for it, my friend! Go for it! And I'll be there for you along the way." Jim shared with me that it would not happen overnight, but rather should evolve through deliberate dialogue and planning.

From that conversation the seeds were planted for Leader's Legacy, the organization I founded in May 2001. And today Jim has become an important part of its growth, serving as a member of the board of directors and continuing to offer much-needed wisdom and counsel. I wouldn't have it any other way.

This principle, where the mentor agrees to join the mentoring partner through such a life-changing transition, is critical. Even if you know where you want to go, it often takes tremendous courage to leave what has become familiar, even if it's only familiarity with misery. There are unknowns that lie ahead and new questions to be addressed. To step out on your own can feel overwhelming and discouraging.

Solomon offers this wise insight: "If one falls down, his friend can help him up. But pity the man who falls and has no one to help him up!" (Ecclesiastes 4:10). From Jim, I needed affirmation that Leader's Legacy was not a foolish notion. It meant so much to know he would be walking along with me during the startup process and afterward, helping me to negotiate the inevitable bumps in the road.

TAKING A SECOND TRACK

Aligning passion with work may not happen overnight, but we have to start somewhere. One useful approach might be to use an assessment tool that is specifically designed to identify these passions. In my consulting work as well as in mentoring, the Birkman Method[5] — a comprehensive personal profile Roger Birkman has developed — is the best resource of this type that I have found. It has helped me to pinpoint issues and possible solutions very quickly. The reason I became sold on it is because the assessment is dynamic — as are individuals — and its findings remain valid even as people grow and change. However, because it is so in-depth, special training is needed to use it effectively.

There are other resources available that come highly recommended, but in general it's important to proceed carefully in the use of any assessment tool because there is a danger of placing a fixed evaluation on someone who will be changing continually and often dramatically over time. For this reason, even though probing questions are not as "scientific," I have found that they can be extremely revealing in a mentoring relationship. They can stimulate ongoing dialogue that proves both enlightening and liberating.

Terry was another friend who was struggling with a career that had become dissatisfying and, frankly, boring. At one time he had felt extremely challenged and rewarded by his job, but as the needs and direction of his organization changed, he found himself doing less and less of the work that fulfilled his passions. More and more of his assignments fell outside his expertise and interests, simply because someone had to do them. Even responsibilities that fit his vocational niche had become so mundane they had a "been there, done that" feel to them.

"Much of the time these days," he confided, "I feel like a Thoroughbred race horse that is being asked to pull a plow. Yes, that can be done, but is that the *best* thing to do?"

One day a good friend called and asked Terry about how his job was going. At first, Terry tried to be politically correct, saying positive things about his work and his organization. But then the friend asked, "If you were guaranteed that you would make all the money you needed and you could do anything you wanted to do, would you continue doing what you're doing?" Terry paused a moment before admitting, "No, I wouldn't."

That simple question ignited his thinking, along with a chain of events that eventually led to a redirection in his career that Terry never would have anticipated. Today he feels as fulfilled as he ever has in more than three decades in his profession.

I usually ask a slightly different question: "If you lived in a perfect world, and money was not an issue, what would you really love to give your life to?" Granted, we don't live in a perfect world, and it seems money will always be an issue. But at least it provokes some honest thought. It might even be that these types of questions have spurred your own thinking.

It's important to emphasize at this point that in addressing the issue of passion, our mentoring role is to foster self-discovery by asking good questions but not necessarily doing things for the partner. The role of mentor is not job placement, although if we hear of a job that could be a good fit, that's fine; it happens sometimes, but that's not our objective. Once we discover that people we are mentoring feel "stuck," we want to challenge them to consider ways they can become "unstuck." That means helping them to find out what they really want to do, serving as a sounding board for their frustrations, and offering helpful insights from our own experience.

But a listening ear can provide only so much comfort. That's why, once I have gotten a clearer picture of what my mentoring partner's passion is, I often suggest taking a "second track" approach. It might be possible to change jobs within the company to one more in line with this passion. However, if that is not a possibility, another option is to "tinker" outside the current work environment — starting on a second track. Taking a trial-and-error approach, people can experiment with any number of alternatives — some of which may prove totally unsatisfactory — without having to cut themselves off from their livelihood.

Let's go back to Skip once again. As we talked, he had expressed his longtime interest in real estate, particularly in interfacing with people to help them find the home of their dreams. Leaving a well-paying executive position with an accounting firm for a very uncertain career in real estate made no practical sense. But I encouraged him to tinker on the side with that line of work, first to see if he truly enjoyed it and, second, to develop an income stream that could make such a transition more viable. It took him two years, but eventually Skip left accounting in the past as he launched a new business in home building and remodeling.

I think of a married couple I was coaching in another city. He was a bank officer and she was an architect, both very accomplished in their professions yet feeling equally stifled. Jeff had the type of personality that has a strong, positive effect on others, but in his administrative role he had few opportunities to interact with people on a meaningful level. Brenda's father had been an architect, and because she was strong in math, most people assumed she was a "chip off the old block" and her career course was set. She had a great love for the arts and was highly creative, but unfortunately her job gave her little outlet to find expression for those aspects of her identity.

As we met and maintained an ongoing dialogue, I encouraged them to explore ways they could pursue their passions either within their current working environments or outside them. For Jeff, there were no options at the bank for fulfilling his longing to work with people, so eventually he switched to a sales career and today loves every minute of it. Brenda was able to redirect her responsibilities at the architectural firm away from structure and into design, and she is fulfilling her passion for the arts by working as a volunteer with community organizations.

Their enthusiasm for work has been rekindled, and the stresses they had endured at home as well as in the workplace have subsided remarkably. It is truly awesome to see how people can flourish when given the opportunity to nurture their strengths and fulfill their passions.

Granted, this second-track approach can be scary, because the familiar — even if unpleasant — can feel more comfortable than the unknown. But sometimes the greatest risk is not taking one, so what's the harm in launching out, at least into the safe environs of open thought and dialogue? I can't tell you how rewarding it is to help mentoring partners make important personal discoveries, learn what their passions are, and start to consider how those might dovetail with vocation. But for mentors there is a second part to this process. We not only need to help our partners find the right place for fulfilling their passions, but we also need to join them on the journey to get there.

CONNECTING TO OUR PASSION

Just as Jim Petersen has walked along the journey with me, I continue to do that with some of the men I mentor. Typically, I have found that an individual's quest to fulfill his or her vocational passion follows three phases:

Discovery

Tinkering

Reality

In a mentoring relationship, working through these phases involves a dialogue that moves progressively from a broad, "over the rainbow" perspective to a far narrower, yet still very intriguing range of realistic alternatives. Let's look at each of these phases individually, seeing how they fit into this journey to find meaning and fulfillment.

Discovery

In this phase, the mentoring partner takes a serious look at, "What am I passionate about? In a perfect world, what is it that I would really love to give my life to?" The response may come quickly, or it may require considerable reflection. There's no time frame for finding an answer.

An important part of this process is free-flowing dialogue, through which more questions are raised than answered initially, but that's okay. As we explore the broad range of possibilities, initially not evaluating how realistic they are, we steadily advance toward solutions and success.

This is why, at the start of such a dialogue, I encourage my mentoring partners to dream, to think in terms of "the sky's the limit," and to extract themselves from the confines of traditional thinking and familiar routines. Otherwise, they might miss a viable alternative that comes to light only through the exercise of their imaginations.

My friend Nolan presents a good example for this phase, as well as for the entire three-phase process. Nolan, a very gifted, loyal senior executive had lost his passion for his role. He was at odds with the direction of his company and its new leadership, and he wanted out. The question was, once he got out, where would he go?

Through our discussions we began uncovering needs and passions that had to be factored into a career move for Nolan. He desired a leadership role where he could influence and motivate people, and he also was looking for flexibility and independence. Almost from the start, we realized this sounded like starting a business of his own, something that had never entered his mind previously.

One of the greatest joys of this discovery phase is that it can take us to the farthest horizons of our imaginations, something most of us have not done since we were children — if then.

Tinkering

Our purpose in this phase is still not to provide solutions or answers, but to probe and to help the mentoring partner probe for possible ways of bringing passion and vocation together. This involves a lot of dialogue and "what ifs." It's a circular process where we mentally march round and round, kicking around ideas for as long as necessary to learn and to evaluate what seems to make sense. But then we have to tinker with the idea. That is, we have to explore the idea to see if it's even feasible in a real world.

Nolan and I had enjoyed talking through the discovery phase, where we soared to the heights. But now it was time to start coming down for a landing and start tinkering. This prompted Nolan to start exploring different avenues, looking at ways his desire for variety, need for independence, and passion to lead people could merge vocationally. His tinkering first involved considering senior management roles with other companies. This was the most comfortable route initially for Nolan because he had been a corporate guy for over twenty years.

Birthing a business is relatively simple. Seeing it survive and thrive is not, however, so Nolan agreed to stay with his company indefinitely, remaining faithful and diligent to his responsibilities while he tinkered with various possibilities outside the corporation. At times the harsh realities of the time and capital necessary to open a new business became somewhat disheartening, but we just continued the dialogue, waiting for the right opportunity to come about. The more he explored and investigated the possibility of starting a business, the more he saw it was not financially feasible.

While none of these options represented the end of his journey, Nolan had identified at least some possibilities that excited him, and these could open doors for other options.

REALITY

In this phase the mentoring partner undertakes a more serious and thorough investigation of viable possibilities, conducting necessary research and fact-finding, and encountering occasional brick walls. Keep in mind that a specific job is not necessarily the central issue. A job provides a context for fulfilling one's passion or calling. Contexts can change, but calling never does.

The situation at Nolan's corporation continued to decline, until one day his position was eliminated. His initial thought was to try latching on with another company, but the substantial severance package he received afforded him the time and financial support needed to establish a consulting business of his own. Longtime contacts in the industry began seeking him on their own. Within a month, he had to start turning customers away. Today Nolan is happier in his work than ever and feels he is now realizing everything he ever desired professionally.

A very important concept to remember is that in the discovery phase, we're "soaring the heights." In the tinkering phase, we're starting to come down for a landing. In the reality phase, the plane has landed. What we're contemplating up in the air will not look the same when we touch down into reality. In Nolan's situation, while he was still up in the air (discovery and tinkering), the idea of starting the kind of business he thought would fit best required several million dollars of startup capital. But when the plane landed (reality), he found that he could start a consulting practice to serve his industry with very little startup capital. As a result, within one month he had more customers at his door than he could handle.

Nolan's "happily ever after" scenario may sound surreal, but keep in mind that his situation involved a three-year process of interacting, exploring, learning, and experimenting. When key elements failed to come together, he wisely stayed put, even though he was anxious to leave his former company. Then, because he had been tinkering with various possibilities, when a real opportunity knocked, he was ready to answer the door.

Please don't conclude that I recommend for everyone who is unhappy at work to automatically start searching for a different company or a new vocation. It is possible to fulfill passions without changing employers. As I have talked with CEOs, they almost unanimously agree that their number-one responsibility is to make and sustain a profit, thus satisfying their shareholders. But when I ask them, "How do you do that?" they acknowledge the obvious: It can only be done through people. For this reason, I think the greatest challenge facing business leaders today is making certain they have the right people in the right jobs. Every day, businesses are losing millions of dollars because of this single issue. If more businesses would commit to the concept of "right person in the right job" by helping people discover their real passion, there is no limit to the positive impact this would have on their bottom lines.

Thankfully, some businesses have recognized the wisdom of this philosophy. The best companies develop their people, understanding it is more efficient and cost-effective to provide a context in which their employees can discover where they fit best. There is no reason any executive cannot ask the same kinds of questions that I ask when I coach or mentor others, so their people can become as productive and fulfilled as possible.

Now that we have explored the issue of passion, in the next chapter we will focus on the second key area of need in a mentoring partner's life: help in easing his or her pain. In the process, you may learn something about dealing with painful issues you are confronting in your own life. But first, I would like you to consider the following questions.

In Pursuit of Life's Passions

1. How would you respond if someone were to ask you, "If you lived in a perfect world, and money was not an issue, what would you really love to give your life to?"

2. From your experience, how common is the problem of men and women working in jobs that fail to fulfill their passions?

3. What is your reaction to the idea of having someone who feels discontented at work starting a second track to explore other possible sources of fulfillment?

4. Have you ever experienced anything like the three-phase process I suggest: discovery, tinkering, and reality? If so, what was it like?

ADVANCING THROUGH ADVERSITY

· ·

PRINCIPLE #5: EFFECTIVE MENTORS ARE
COMFORTERS WHO SHARE THE LOAD.

· ·

*W*hen was the last time you really felt pain? I don't mean stubbing your toe on the bedpost or seeing your favorite team lose the big game. I'm talking about real pain — physical or emotional — that seemed like it would never go away. What was it like? How did it feel?

The reason I ask is because acknowledging pain and attempting to address it in a meaningful way is a key component of the mentoring process. Just as a mentoring partner comes to us with the invitation to "Help me with my passion," as I discussed in the last chapter, in many cases he or she also brings to the table another spoken or implied request: "Help me with my pain."

I will never forget the first time I met with Tripp. As we sat down over dinner, it was obvious he was dealing with a tremendous amount of stress. We started by talking about how globalization had affected the company where he worked as a sales executive. Foreign competition was beating them on almost every front. He commented on how dramatically his particular industry had changed.

Then I decided to shift the focus from the company to Tripp, to try to identify the tension I could see in his face. I asked him if all of this job stress was affecting his personal life. "Oh, absolutely!" he replied. It was as if that single question opened the floodgates.

Tripp explained that he had worked with this company for nearly twenty years. It had been his first job out of college and for the most part he had enjoyed the family-oriented working environment. He had contributed significantly to the company's growth during that time. But with the changes in the industry, the overall tone of the company took a dramatic turn as well. Instead of an attitude of "the employees matter most," it had shifted to a dog-eat-dog, whatever-it-takes-to-survive atmosphere. As a result, despite his consistently high performance and years of loyalty, he had been adversely affected by staffing and policy changes, including seeing his compensation cut almost in half while his responsibilities were increased.

The adversity at work was having an equally negative impact on his home life. His marriage of sixteen years was troubled, and his wife had threatened to leave him. Hoping to salvage the relationship, they were undergoing professional counseling. Emotionally, Tripp's spirits were being propped up by antidepressants. He had discontinued his physical fitness regimen months earlier, and his body was beginning to signal this neglect.

Despite the ill treatment he was receiving from his company, he felt bound to hang on, motivated by his loyalty and desperately hoping for the best. Unfortunately, it was painfully clear that "the best" would still be a long time in coming, if at all. If anything, the situation seemed to worsen by the day.

Tripp admitted he had lost his passion for his career but didn't see a way out. His confidence had fallen to an all-time low, and he was so stuck he did not know how to begin looking for another job. What can we do to help a guy like Tripp?

As we have already seen in the previous chapters, one of the mentor's primary roles for the mentoring partner is to serve as a confidant — a trusted friend who caringly gets into the partner's world by inviting the partner into his or her own world. During times of suffering and pain, however, the mentor must assume another role as well. Sometimes the pain of everyday life becomes too great a burden for one person to handle. An effective mentor then "changes hats" to serve as comforter as well, someone willing to walk with the mentoring partner through the winds and waves of adversity.

Being a comforter involves far more than simply responding in a sympathetic manner, although that is part of it. When someone is bowed down under a load of personal pain and stress, the mentor can step in to help in carrying the load, sharing the burden. You can see an analogy for this at the local sports and fitness club. No matter how dedicated and accomplished, weightlifters always need a spotter in case the load gets too heavy and falls on them, resulting in a serious injury. A mentor is like such a spotter, ready to respond if the load of pain becomes too heavy to lift alone.

One of the values we provide as mentors is that we have traveled further along in the journey through life. We have confronted many of the same struggles our mentoring partners are facing, including workplace pressures, tensions in the home, broken relationships, bad habits, the death of a friend or loved one, financial woes, unfulfilled passions, or anxiety about the future. What did you learn through those times of adversity? And how did you find comfort and hope as you went through them? You can speak to your mentoring partner about your own experiences and offer comfort in a manner similar to how you were comforted. But it's not about giving advice — it's about being there, extending compassion, listening, serving, and being available when needed.

AVOIDING PAIN, OR EMBRACING IT?

We live in a society that specializes in pain avoidance. It seems there is a pill or remedy for virtually any ailment. If not, it's highly probable that something will be available soon. Alcohol and drug abuse reportedly have risen to all-time highs (no pun intended) as people seek to escape all manner of psychological and emotional pain, regardless of whether the source can be traced to an earlier time in one's life or just the inevitable struggles of daily life and work. And many areas of the entertainment industry are booming as men, women, and young people hunt for diversions from real-life hardships.

But is pain something we should avoid or stuff inside where we hopefully can ignore it at all costs? You might want to pause a moment before answering. Some years ago, Dr. Paul Brand and Philip Yancey wrote an intriguing book called *Pain: The Gift Nobody Wants*. Brand, who has devoted his life to treating patients afflicted with leprosy and other diseases that cause insensitivity to pain, notes the irony that, "while most of us seek out pharmacists and doctors in search of relief from pain, these people live in constant peril due to pain's *absence*."

Drawing from his own experience, both as a physician and as a person living in a world that seems bent on inflicting pain of endless varieties, Brand has concluded, "My own encounters with pain . . . as well as the specter of painlessness, have produced in me an attitude of wonder and appreciation. I do not desire, and cannot even imagine, a life without pain. For that reason I accept the challenge of trying to restore balance to how we think about pain. . . . We can learn to cope, and even to triumph."[1]

In reality, adversity is as much a part of everyday life as those events and pursuits that bring us happiness. Because we can't hide from adversity, doesn't it make sense to deal with it directly and, if possible, productively? Everyone hurts at one time or another, and talking about pain is part of the natural process of building trust and deepening relationships. If we ignore pain, mentoring relationships won't advance beyond the superficial and cannot last for very long.

David Seltzer, the writer of the film *Dragonfly*, starring Kevin Costner, says it very well in a commentary about the drama: "I think that human beings bond through their pain. It's common to all of us. I don't think we connect very well when we're in a joyful mood, because everybody's joy is so idiosyncratic, and so transient, and passes so quickly. But I do find that the human condition connects very easily when we understand one another's pain."

Earlier I mentioned the film project I was involved in when I met Jim Petersen, who would later become my mentor. As we were discussing the big ideas we wanted to communicate through our video series on mentoring others, Jim stunned all of us by suggesting the topic of suffering and adversity. He explained that no one wants to talk about this issue, as if ignoring it will make it go away. Instead, we avoid the subject entirely, deny that it exists, or try to "fix it" as quickly as possible. Eventually, we agreed with Jim that the issue of pain had to be addressed in our film to accomplish our ultimate objective, although I think we still retained a degree of discomfort with the idea.

Since that time I have thought a lot about pain and about why we try so hard not to deal with it, both in our own lives and in the lives of people around us. For one thing, frankly, it's just too painful.

We would prefer to take two aspirin and call the doctor in the morning, but only if necessary. Adversity also can be ugly. No one enjoys looking at shriveled plants — or shriveled lives. But perhaps our greatest reason for trying to avoid even the discussion of pain is because we don't know how to deal with it. It's often hard to know how to cope with our own pain, let alone someone else's.

A heartening, behind-the-scenes story about Phil Ford, a former University of North Carolina All-American basketball player and NBA star, and his former coach at UNC, the renowned Dean Smith, is instructive. David Chadwick, in his book *The 12 Leadership Principles of Dean Smith*, tells how Smith intervened when it was revealed that Ford was fighting a losing battle with alcohol.

Chadwick quotes Ford, who asserts, "Coach Smith saved my life. It was like he was saying to me, 'Hey, I'm here for you. It's going to be me and you. You and I will solve this problem together.'" Smith's gesture of support gave Ford hope and a renewed sense of purpose as they confronted his alcoholism together. "That's the way friends act," Chadwick writes. "They forgive our human frailties and reach out to help us when we need it."[2]

This principle is not the private domain of basketball coaches. In the midst of adversity, this also is what mentors do. With a mentor who is a comforter, there is no need for mentoring partners to conceal, repress, or avoid their pain. Instead, they deal with it directly, knowing "it's going to be me and you."

HAVING A HEART OF COMPASSION

We typically make someone else's pain more complicated than necessary. We want to give advice and offer a way to resolve the problem. But what we really need is a heart of compassion.

A three-year study by the CompassionLab, a joint project of the University of Michigan Business School and the University of British Columbia, researched how different organizations addressed pain and demonstrated compassion with the people who worked for them. The researchers studied how compassion had "a direct impact on how quickly and effectively people in those organizations were able to recover from tragic events."

The article in *Harvard Business Review* states, "You can help individuals and companies begin to heal by taking actions that demonstrate your own compassion, thereby unleashing a compassionate response." The authors point out, "When people know they can bring their pain to the office, they no longer have to expend energy trying to ignore or suppress it, and they can more easily and effectively get back to work. . . . Conversely, when you expect people to stifle their emotions, they don't know how and where to direct their energies and it's very difficult for them to figure out how to focus at work."[3]

This holds true for mentoring as well. When we demonstrate a heart of compassion, our mentoring partners can feel free to bring their pain to us. Many times this will allow the partners to start the difficult but necessary process of moving out of the hurtful past and painful present into the promising future.

In Romans 12:15, Paul wrote that we should "rejoice with those who rejoice; mourn with those who mourn." Another translation states we are to "weep with those who weep" (NASB). The word *compassion* literally means "with feeling," and when the people we mentor are overcome with intense feelings — the kinds that tie their stomachs in knots — it helps when we can show how deeply we are moved and respond to them with similar feelings.

Maybe you're one of those people who says, "Well, I can't do that. I'm not a very sensitive person." All I can say is welcome to the club. I have to admit it: I'm not a naturally merciful type of guy. I care about people, but when it comes to showing compassion, don't try using me as a good example. Compounding the problem somewhat is my background in sports medicine. Because I tend to interpret actions I observe based on my training in biomechanics, when I see someone fall, I can tell fairly accurately whether they have been hurt seriously. And if they aren't hurt badly, I tend to discount the injury entirely.

One afternoon I was walking with a friend outside my office building. A woman stumbled on the sidewalk and fell right in front of me. By perceiving the incident through my biomechanical grid, I could see she had a "safe" fall and wasn't hurt, but probably was a bit embarrassed. As I expected, she immediately got back up, so I continued walking and talking as if nothing had happened. My friend, however, a far more merciful soul than I, stopped immediately to offer some compassion and make sure the woman was doing okay.

Suddenly, I became the one embarrassed by my own insensitivity, especially because my friend was a young man I had been mentoring. "Do as I say, not as I do" is not a good philosophy for mentoring, or for life. I don't think I'd ever find myself a candidate for the Mr. Sensitivity award. However, as years have passed and I have witnessed how much pain we all face, I'm being challenged more and more to have a heart of compassion, especially with my family and those I mentor. The good news is that this does not require a major personality makeover. Mastering a compassionate approach for helping our mentoring partners deal with their pain can be as simple as recognizing that little things matter, as having a listening ear, and as understanding the importance of just being there, as we will see in the sections that follow.

LITTLE THINGS MATTER

When there doesn't appear to be a quick-fix available, we typically feel at a loss regarding what to do. Maybe we should take a lesson from Lucy, one of Anne's close friends. My dad's death shattered me emotionally. After spending my teenage and college years virtually estranged from him, we had mended our relationship and forged a friendship I could not have imagined possible. So when he died, it seemed as if I had lost a part of my own body. The day of the funeral, while we were busily involved in arrangements, our friend Lucy came by to help with preparing food for our family and friends who came by to visit. (Until that time, I could never understand when I saw movie portrayals of people having a feast after a funeral. If you're grieving, I had thought, why would you want to eat?) When Lucy saw me, she didn't waste a lot of words. She just said, with great compassion, "Dave, I'm so sorry." Then she quietly went to work.

Lucy obviously was concerned for me and for my family, but understood that the time for words would come later. She was right. I'm a person who likes a lot of time alone, and I was deep into my own world, processing my pain. I had no desire to talk to anyone, and she honored that.

Strangely enough, as I watched Lucy prepare the food for us, it comforted me. She was showing how much she cared, without having to express it verbally. On that day — to borrow a phrase I learned from my mentor Jim — Lucy was "short on words, long on service." To this day, I am always blessed when I think of her servant's spirit. She was right about something else: I could not believe how hungry I was right after the funeral. I might have set a world record for the amount of food I consumed!

Next to the trauma of my dad dying, nothing about those difficult days stands out for me more than what Lucy did for us. Her
example, demonstrating that little things matter, will remain with me
forever. She didn't do anything flashy, just attended to the simple
matter that after the funeral there would be a lot of hungry people.
Little things can have a big impact. Perhaps she understood so well
what to do because she had lost her dad years earlier.

The reason I say we get too complicated in trying to deal with pain
others are facing is that it's not necessary to "fix it." People are tired of
people offering quick fixes, even if they are hurting deeply. With good
intentions, we desperately want to do or say something profound, but
sometimes to help the most, we don't need to say or do anything other
than being available. When people are feeling pain, little things —
whether they involve inauspiciously preparing food, running errands, or
just being physically present — often matter most. What they may need
the most is just to know that we care and that we are there for them.

The CompassionLab article "Leading in Times of Trauma" tells
about the dean of a divinity school who experienced the unexpected
death of a close relative. Reporting that the dean received the greatest comfort from a couple who simply came to his home and wept
with him, the authors note, "To this day he remembers their very
presence as a powerful moment of healing."[4]

Sometimes helping people work through their pain can be as
simple as shedding a few genuine tears.

A LISTENING HEART

Most of us are not trained therapists, but that doesn't shield us from
people caught up in pain. Occasionally, a situation may arise where

professional therapy is warranted, but I have found that often what people need most is a listening heart, an understanding look, perhaps a gentle, reassuring touch, and words used sparingly. As Proverbs 17:28 points out, "Even a fool is thought wise if he keeps silent, and discerning if he holds his tongue."

In the early '90s, one of my major goals was to formulate a strategy for developing the next generation of leaders for the organization I was with at the time. Until then, most of my mentoring relationships had been with peers — Baby Boomers and even guys who were older than me.

The Cold War had ended and our nation was entering a new era when change was constant and uncertainty was pervasive. I wanted to gain a sense of where our society was heading, so I began to research an emerging generation that sociologists had labeled "Generation X" — basically young adults who had been born between 1965 and 1980. What I learned took me completely by surprise. I discovered a generation immersed in pain, struggling with great uncertainty, exhibiting little hope, and crying out for mentors. They desperately wanted someone who could provide a road map to follow, some way to find order in the midst of their chaotic lives — an order that made sense in an everyday, practical way. They wanted not only to be heard, but also to be understood.

What shocked me even more was the great chasm between these young people, who were entering the workplace for the first time, and the older, more seasoned people, who could serve as their mentors. I was thirty-seven at the time and even in my organization, I was one of its youngest leaders. Most of our volunteers were much older and seemed tragically out of touch with this new generation.

The behavior of Gen-Xers did not fit our grid. It seemed

rebellious to the status quo, to authority, to institutionalism. Many people called them "slackers" because they did not embrace the work ethic of the Baby Boomer and pre-World War II generations. When I started my business career in the late 1970s and early 1980s, loyalty to your company and the idea of retiring one day with a gold watch were still predominant values. However, Gen-Xers could not have held less regard for gold watches and corporate loyalty. All they wanted to do was survive, and because of the broken relationships they had already experienced, they had little confidence about doing that.

Ironically, even though my organization had long placed a high priority on mentoring, we consistently failed to connect with members of this generation that needed so badly to be mentored. Accustomed to mentoring individuals who did what you told them to do, performed assignments given to them, showed up on time, and "dressed for success," many of our trained mentors suddenly found themselves unable to relate to young people who opposed such structure. The Gen-Xers refused to "make the formations."

My challenge became clear: to learn how to understand the men and women of Generation X and how to mentor them most effectively. However, I wanted to do more than read and gather research. I wanted to test my thinking and intuition through the laboratory of real-life experience. My philosophy has always been that if we don't model what we are teaching others, we are not worth following, and I wanted to be able to speak from firsthand knowledge, not theory. If you make a practice of teaching above where you're living, eventually you will find yourself out of touch with where people really are.

So I began teaching a Bible class for singles at a church, with my objective being to engage with Gen-Xers on a personal level. What they showed me was pain — lives torn by broken promises, broken relationships, and broken dreams. On the outside, they all looked good. They seemed so "together." But as I got to know them, I realized that their lives were filled with turmoil and hurt. One of their greatest desires was for mentors who could walk with them in their pain. They wanted to be heard, to feel that someone was truly listening when they talked about their struggles. Even more importantly, they desperately wanted to be understood. They were looking for real people, people who cared, people who would just take the time to listen and not throw out simplistic, pat solutions to problems.

Victor was one of my first Gen-X mentoring experiences. I have to admit he stretched my learning curve. Here was a young guy starting out in his career, rebellious to the "establishment." He definitely had no interest in driving his father's Oldsmobile, as the TV commercial suggested years ago. He looked great on the outside — very street smart. Years later, he confessed that he had told me about every objectionable activity he was involved with — drugs, alcohol, immoral relationships, late nights out — just to test me and see if I cared, or if I would judge him. Determined to accept him where he was, not where I felt he was supposed to be, I didn't flinch when he told me about his wild behavior, even when I personally disapproved.

Apparently, I must have passed the test because Victor kept meeting with me and, over time, revealed how much he was hurting inside. I found he was fairly typical of his generation, and our times together were truly a two-way learning experience. Sometimes it seemed as if our mentoring relationship was not going anywhere, but that was not how he viewed it. He wanted to be listened to and to feel that someone finally understood him. For him, I filled the bill. When he started sharing unreservedly and when the tears he had been holding in for so long began to flow, I knew we were making progress.

When we first started meeting, Victor's career was a mess and headed nowhere. Today, however, he is a successful businessman and the envy of many of his peers. It has been such a great joy to see how he has flourished in life. Even though he has not yet "arrived," at least he is well on the way.

My own mentoring relationship with Jim Petersen was such a great help during that time because of the tremendous insights he provided from his vast international, cross-cultural experience. He taught me how to relate to people living in contexts that were unfamiliar, which was definitely the case for an older Baby Boomer trying to relate to a Gen-Xer.

In addition, the way Jim modeled a listening heart with me as I went through my vocational struggles enabled me to do the same with Victor. Unlike the structured approach to mentoring that I had learned from my organization, I remembered that Jim had not brought an agenda into our relationship, electing instead just to listen attentively, make a few notes, offer an occasional comment, and pose some questions. Understanding how he had helped me to make sense of the pain in my life, I was able to do the same for Victor.

JUST BEING THERE

The real heart of a mentor is just being there for someone. As I have already noted, people long to be heard and listened to, to feel that even when struggling with some kind of adversity, there is somebody who understands. Believe me, sometimes your simple presence and willingness to listen is the greatest gift you could possibly offer to a hurting person.

Recently, I was talking with some teenagers, including my sons,

Paul and Aaron, and my daughter, Sarah. Our discussion covered a variety of topics, so I asked them, "When you're going through a tough time, how do you deal with pain?" Remember, these were teenagers, not yet very experienced in life, but they all reached the same conclusion: "It always feels better to talk about it with a close friend, someone I really trust."

When I asked them to tell me what such a friend might look like, their descriptions did not call to mind a highly educated, well-seasoned executive, therapist, or counselor. Instead, they simply described someone who really cares, is willing to listen, and is available to walk alongside them through their time of difficulty. This is not to minimize the importance of trained professionals with the expertise to assist people dealing with profound difficulties or clinical issues. I spent a number of years in the medical field and have great respect and admiration for psychiatrists and psychologists, but studies have shown that the majority of people who go for counseling really don't need it. What they need is a compassionate friend, someone who will listen without being judgmental and who won't "tell the world."

What if you can't relate to the pain your mentoring partner is facing? You can just listen, show compassion, and simply *be there*. This is what a friend of mine did some years ago: Ted told me about answering a phone call one evening. He recognized a familiar voice and said lightheartedly, "Hi, Darren! How are you doing?"

There was no lightness in Darren's voice. With halting words that made it evident that he was fighting back tears, he simply said, "Ted, I need a friend."

Ted had mentored Darren some years earlier, but since that time they had seen each other only occasionally. Darren and his wife had experienced some conflict in the past, but Ted had no idea whether marital problems had prompted his friend's call. Hearing an edge of desperation in Darren's voice, Ted tried to be as reassuring as possible. "Darren, I'm your friend. How can I help you?" For the next several minutes, all Darren could do was repeat the words he had said at the start: "I need a friend."

Finally, Ted persuaded him to meet at a nearby restaurant the following day. When they got together, Darren was able to say, "Ted, I've messed up. I don't know what to do." Gradually, he revealed that his wife had left him and was filing for divorce, but Ted knew there had to be more to the story than that.

Slowly and reluctantly, Darren confided that for more years than he could remember, he had been struggling with a secret addiction. For a long time he had succeeded in keeping it concealed, but recently his wife had found out and it had devastated her. Disconsolate and unwilling to forgive, she had packed the same day and moved out. Then, with eyes filled with hurt and loneliness, Darren asked, "Will you still be my friend?" Ted assured him that he would remain his friend and be there for him as he worked through this painful time.

Remember my story about Tripp to start off this chapter? Today his circumstances are dramatically — and happily — different. The rift in his marriage has healed and the relationship is growing stronger every day. After more than twenty years, he left his employer and today is in his element vocationally. He pinches himself sometimes, still finding it hard to believe that he has fallen into the career of his dreams. While his current company is owned by another person, Tripp is an active shareholder and has complete freedom and flexibility to carry out his responsibilities as he sees fit — and he does that very well.

What did I do to help? In one sense, not a lot. I just did a few little things, like listening and being there when he needed me. But for Tripp, that was all that was necessary.

Seems too simple, doesn't it? Recognizing that little things matter, offering a listening heart, and just being there. They may not seem like a lot, but when extended to someone in pain, they may seem like the greatest treasure in the world.

FINDING MEANING IN PAIN

The fascinating thing about pain is that we can't just make it all better. When my children suffer physical hurts or become sick with the flu, they have to heal on their own. It is assuring as parents to know that there are little things Anne and I can do that make a big difference. We can put a bandage on the wound, give them some medicine, or take them to the doctor's office. We can be there for them, listening and comforting them. Often, that is also the very best we can do for our mentoring partners.

One other critical thing we can do as comforters, however, is to help people try to find meaning in their pain. Through my years of working with people, I have found that most of the time, they are looking for reasons for their intense pain. Think about it: What's the first question we often ask when we're experiencing pain from tragic or unfortunate circumstances? "Why?" Where is the purpose — or meaning — in our pain?

We recently attended a funeral of a friend whose husband died. He was a man only in his mid-thirties who had kept himself in tremendous physical shape. A very gifted and talented individual, he had lost a brave battle with cancer. As Anne and I embraced his wife, she asked, "Why?" Anne held her and listened, but had no answers to give. We couldn't change the circumstances, but over the weeks that followed, my wife was able to provide comfort for this woman as she wrestled with this question and many others.

In his book *Man's Search for Meaning*, Viktor Frankl explains it was this sense of meaning that enabled some people — including himself — to survive the horrors of the German concentration camps during World War II. He points out that while we cannot always control our circumstances, we can control our attitudes toward them and strive to find some sense of meaning in the pain.[5]

Even though we can attempt to help mentoring partners in trying to find a reason for their pain, this does not necessarily mean they will find the answer — or that they need to do so. As a matter of fact, this quest to answer "Why?" may raise even more questions. But having someone to walk alongside you when the load of pain becomes unbearable makes all the difference. Even if the search for meaning in our pain turns empty, eventually healing can take place. It's gratifying for a mentor to be used as one of the instruments for that healing.

Pain was an everyday reality for me as a boy growing up. In addition to my poor relationship with my father, our family wrestled with financial problems, particularly after he retired from the military. We all found it difficult to adjust to civilian life. It was not until my adult years that I learned to find meaning in the pain of my early years, recognizing how adversity could be put to positive use in shaping my character. Facing my personal demons and learning to overcome them has molded me into a comforter myself.

Paul in the Bible has served as a tremendous inspiration for me in this respect. He experienced much adversity and pain, and like many of us, searched for meaning in his pain. I think in large measure he found that meaning. This is why he could write, "Praise be to the God and Father of our Lord Jesus Christ, the Father of compassion and the God of all comfort, who comforts us in all our troubles, so that we can comfort those in any trouble with the comfort we ourselves have received from God" (2 Corinthians 1:3-4).

Doesn't that make sense? The comfort that we receive when we are in pain helps us in processing and finding healing for our pain. And then we can use this comfort to help others in pain.

It's important to remember that as a mentor, sooner or later you will have to deal with pain that no one wants to acknowledge. It may be messy, but helping mentoring partners confront it can be immensely rewarding. So learn to be a comforter. Stand with people in their pain. Walk with them in their adversity. Weep with them in their suffering. Share your own pain. Be real. And most of all, be short on words and long on service.

Having looked at the first two "Ps" that mentoring partners find so perplexing, in the next chapter we will look at the third: *priorities*. In a world with so many demands, so many people and things tugging at us, how can we help our partners find balance and release from controlling pressures? We will look at this, but first I would like you to consider the following questions.

Prescriptions for Pain Relief

1. How did you answer my question about the last time you really felt pain? What was the pain like?

2. What is your typical reaction to pain and adversity? Do you try to avoid it, stuff it deep inside, or ignore it, hoping it will go away? Or have you learned that there are positives to be gained as we go through the hardships of life? What happens when you "stuff," or repress, your pain?

3. How do you typically respond when someone you know is going through a painful experience? Are you "short on words, long on service," or the opposite?

4. How do you feel about the idea that part of being a mentor means being willing to walk with a mentoring partner through pain and adversity, even if it means not being able to provide a "quick fix"?

LET YOUR VALUES FILTER BE YOUR GUIDE

· ·

PRINCIPLE #6: EFFECTIVE MENTORS HELP TURN

PERSONAL VALUES INTO PRACTICE.

· ·

would like to introduce you to a man I'll call Pinball. I'm giving him this nickname because I met someone once who described himself and his life as being like the ball in a pinball machine. Like that shiny, metal ball bouncing from bumper to bumper, constantly darting from one direction to another, sometimes racking up points and sometimes rolling into the gutter, Pinball was out of control.

His business was successful and he obviously loved every bit of what he was doing in his company, but poor Pinball was experiencing tremendous stress. As he described for me all the activities and opportunities clamoring for his attention, in his business as well as in other areas of his life, it became clear that he was afflicted with what some people might term "the tyranny of the urgent." He floundered helplessly from one crisis to another, without any semblance of order or a cohesive plan for how he should approach these demands and responsibilities.

The root cause of Pinball's turmoil was that his priorities were desperately skewed, causing his life to be out of balance. As he discussed the pressures and pain of his life, I could clearly understand comparing his life to a pinball machine. As a kid, I had loved playing pinball. Sometimes my determination to rack up points became so intense I pushed the machine a little too hard. Guess what happened? I caused the game to "TILT," shutting it down. After hearing Pinball's story, it was evident to me that this guy's life also was on the verge of going TILT.

That is exactly what happened. One by one, parts of his life that he cherished started crumbling. The business fell on hard times and Pinball scrambled to try to hold it together. His marriage, already suffering from years of neglect as he poured himself into the company, worsened as he spent even more time at work. Through all of this, he contracted a serious physical ailment. My friend Pinball was fortunate to have his professional life aligned with his passion, but he had gone too far. He had placed so much emphasis on his career, the other things in his life that also were important to him had become overshadowed and, in comparison, seemed almost inconsequential.

Stress and pain — emotional and physical — finally got his attention, but by then it was almost too late. His problems, of course, had not materialized overnight. It was much more subtle. As he became engrossed in his vocational passion, Pinball slowly and subconsciously had sacrificed other priorities: his family, physical and emotional health, hobbies, and time with friends. Completely out of balance, he teetered on the verge of losing everything he held dear.

As I have mentored men over the years, I have heard many stories similar to this. Most are not as extreme but are troubling just the same. Along with addressing the areas of passion and pain, another of a mentor's most important roles is to help mentoring partners establish and maintain priorities. Frankly, many people have never taken the time to think through what is most important to them. They simply *react* to circumstances they confront, rather than taking a *proactive* approach. If you were to ask people, "What are the top priorities in your life?" they might be hard-pressed to give you a definitive answer.

Not long ago MasterCard ran a series of media ads and commercials that showed the cost of participating in various activities, such as sporting events, cultural gatherings, or vacations. They displayed the different costs, and then as each commercial ended, they showed something that was "priceless." As mentors, we want to help our partners to identify what matters the most to them — what would qualify as *priceless* in their minds — and then to help them to turn their personal values into practice, not just theory. It's not fun being a Pinball.

THE VALUE OF VALUES

So what is the function of values? What is their benefit for us, particularly in a mentoring context? Basically, established values offer three benefits: First, values act as a filter that determines priorities. Second, priorities provide balance, a sense of order and control that so many of us long to have. Third, the more balanced our lives are, the happier and more productive we are.

It's important to note that values and priorities are distinct; having one does not necessarily mean you have the other. Pinball, for example, valued his marriage and other aspects of his personal life, but he let his work crowd them out. The challenge is to articulate and affirm what our values are, then take steps to honor these values in a practical sense — in other words, assign priorities to them. But before we can establish specific priorities, we must first have a clear understanding of what our values actually are. They serve as a framework for distinguishing "could do" opportunities from "should do" opportunities.

James M. Kouzes and Barry Z. Posner, authors of *The Leadership Challenge* (Jossey-Bass, 1987) affirm the importance of values in a chapter for *The Drucker Foundation: The Leader of the Future*. They state that people are looking for leaders who are credible, and one way of establishing credibility is by clearly communicating personal values: "People expect their leaders to stand for something and to have the courage of their convictions. If leaders are not clear about what they believe in, they are more likely to change their position with every fad or opinion poll. Therefore, the first milestone on the journey to leadership credibility is clarity of personal values."[1]

The same applies to mentors and mentoring partners. Without personal values, we're going to be all over the map, "driven and tossed by the wind," as the Bible says in James 1:6 (NASB). Values are critical because they give us a sense of balance, a means for separating not only the bad from the good, but also the good from the best.

My years of mentoring have shown me that balance is always a major issue and that mentoring partners desperately long for it. It's a concern that everybody brings up, often in the first meeting. But this does not mean they need a time-management course. For them, the issue is much deeper. They want assistance in attaining the things most important to them, many of which don't fit on a "to do" list. These are things like happiness; contentment; successful relationships; achievement; making a difference in the world; physical, mental, and emotional well-being; significance; respect; esteem; and acceptance. No personal organizing system can teach you how to schedule happiness between 2:30 and 3:00 P.M. or how to be a difference-maker from 11 A.M. to noon.

Once we clearly understand what we genuinely value in life — not what someone else says we should value — we can start prioritizing our actions and activities to align with those values. I call this a "values filter," a way of sifting through the myriad choices and opportunities that confront us, allowing only those endeavors and pursuits that align with and support our values to pass through. Picture a huge funnel with everything being poured into the wide end, but at the narrow end, having a specially designed filter to screen out anything that conflicts with your predetermined values.

Most bookstores and libraries boast dozens of books on organizational values. Virtually every organization today has (or is in the process of writing) formal values statements. Unfortunately, many businesses have treated values statements like a fad. They display them in elaborate frames on walls or file them away in desk drawers, but they fail to live them out. James C. Collins, in his books *Built to Last* (HarperBusiness, 1996) and *Good to Great* (HarperBusiness, 2001), has underscored the benefits of values in the organizations he has studied. Companies that hold true to clearly articulated and understood values outlast those without a system of values to govern their operations. Stated values help provide answers to the questions of what, how, and why things are done.

If values are critical for organizations, they are even more crucial for individuals. Organizations can change, get new ownership, go out of business, or merge. If they have values statements, those can be rewritten. Personal values, however, serve as an unchanging anchor that provides stability even when all around us seems in flux. And organizational values, after all, are nothing more than reflections of the personal values held by their leaders.

One of the best ways mentors can assist their mentoring partners is to help them identify and establish their personal values. People who live more balanced lives are happier and more productive, partly because they don't have to wrestle with the subconscious guilt of expending too much time and energy in one important area of their lives and neglecting another. Guided by what we value most, life becomes more fulfilling and we can accomplish more. The alternative — trying to live without keeping our values foremost in our minds — will result only in chaos and frustration.

And keep in mind that some of the individuals we mentor will be people who one day, as business executives, civic leaders, and public officials, will help shape the values of their companies, communities, and country.

This is not to say that defining personal priorities promises a perfectly balanced life. Not at all. Like the circus performer walking the high wire, we find that keeping balance can be accomplished only one step at a time. We will always feel tension in keeping our priorities in order, but that should not discourage us. Some days we will feel we have everything in the proper order; other days we'll be convinced that our lives could not become more jumbled. It's a universal challenge. I once heard a speaker comment that the only person he ever saw truly in balance was someone who was in the process of moving from one extreme to the other. When we recognize those things we value most, we can make adjustments to ensure that they don't remain neglected for long.

Ozzie, a good friend of mine, is a senior executive for a company in my city. Not married, he would devote many of his nonworking hours to his personal passion, being a musician. For years, in his free time he was producing beautiful melodies. When he first experienced the fulfillment of mentoring someone, he added another personal value: investing in people. Because Ozzie saw no reason to curtail his musical pursuits either, he suddenly was confronted with a conflict of interests in the most literal sense. By passing these and other activities through his values filter, however, he was able to resolve this tension by reordering his priorities to allot sufficient time for both mentoring and music.

Today Ozzie feels freed from the pressures of trying to squeeze every demand into his life. It's one of those win-win situations for everyone involved. His employers respect him tremendously and appreciate his work — and he does a lot of it. However, he labors diligently and efficiently to keep his job from consuming all his time. He always makes certain to allocate time for both mentoring and music because these pursuits fulfill him the most. And because his work does not impede him from pursuing these passions, Ozzie finds his job more fulfilling than ever.

This is why helping our mentoring partners seriously examine their values so they can assign appropriate priorities to their work and other areas of their lives is so critical.

DISCOVERING AND EMBRACING OUR VALUES

How do we formulate our personal values — the priceless dimensions of our lives upon which we want to concentrate our attention and energy? First, it's important to understand that values come from the heart; they are a reflection of who we are, not of what we do.

Some of our values come virtually built in; they are imparted to us through culture. This can include those formed from a national or ethnic framework, as well as those passed on to us through family, friends, and peers.

In a *Business Week* article called "Rethinking the Rat Race," Diane Brady shows how work holds a strong priority in the minds of Americans, which is in sharp contrast to the mindset of workers in other nations. According to the article, people in Germany, France, and Italy take from thirty-five to more than forty vacation days per year on average, and even in Japan, South Korea, Canada, and Britain, business and professional people enjoy twenty-five days or more of vacation time. The average American, however, manages to squeeze only about twelve vacation days into a given year.[2]

This helps to explain why business and professional people in Europe think it quite routine to take several weeks or even a month for "holiday," detaching themselves totally from work, while most Americans struggle to break away for even a long weekend. There obviously is an extreme difference in the value placed on work in different cultures. As I heard one European businessman express it, "Americans live to work; Europeans work to live."

A friend was in a South American country, discussing with his hosts the difference in time orientation between United States businesspeople and those in Hispanic societies. Americans on the whole place a premium on punctuality, while their Latin American counterparts did not seem to share such a sense of urgency, my friend noted. One of the Latino businessmen laughed, "Amigo, that is just our culture!" Another businessman expanded on that thought: "Culture is nothing more than values that are handed down from one generation to another." Time, he explained, simply is not valued in the same way in many Latin American cultures as it is in the United States.

These examples show how a national or ethnic culture can affect personal values, but values also can be shaped through families. For instance, values imparted through the home can range from attitudes toward regular weekly worship to how often you bathe. And as we all know, the teenage culture can have a startling impact on values, the manifestations of which can change drastically from year to year.

But these values are determined largely by external influences. As we engage in mentoring, we are more concerned about personal, individual values. Unlike values that are basically "inherited," personal values are shaped by three primary factors: crises, passions, and needs.

FINDING VALUES THROUGH CRISIS

If you want to test your values and priorities sometime, consider how you respond in a crisis. Have you ever had a time when you felt so inundated by commitments that you were convinced you could not handle even one more thing? You had deadlines to meet, appointments to keep, and responsibilities to fulfill — and no idea how you could handle them all. Yet if the phone had rung and someone had informed you of an emergency — perhaps an accident involving someone dear to you, or a serious illness — wouldn't you have dropped all the "important" things so you could attend to something or someone that was higher on your priority list?

This was the case for me the day my dad died. Sales calls, paperwork, monthly quotas — everything ceased to have any importance while my family and I dealt with our grief and arrangements leading up to his funeral. And for almost every one of us, all nonessentials were put on hold on September 11 when we learned about the terrorist attacks on the World Trade Center and the Pentagon, along with developments that followed. Stunned and numbed by the unthinkable, no one I knew did much of anything productive for days; some people took weeks to get their lives and routines back to normal.

One of the positives of the 9-11 tragedies was that it caused a lot of us to examine our priorities, perhaps for the first time. The conclusion many of us reached was that nothing was more important than our families — not our dream jobs, our long-awaited vacations, or the fates of our favorite sports teams. We learned an important truth: Values are not truly values unless we firmly hold to them when it's inconvenient, when other, more pressing demands clamor for our attention.

FINDING VALUES IN OUR PASSIONS

Our passions — those pursuits that we love to do, the things that provide us with the greatest sense of fulfillment — also go a long way in determining our personal values. For many of us, the work we do is certainly a central part of this. As we gain a clearer understanding of what our inner passions are, we can ascertain whether our vocations complement or clash with our values.

As I have explained earlier, the value I place on developing people — seeking to influence them positively and to lead them — eventually led to a major career change. I have a strong creative bent, and writing this book is one by-product of that, also spurred by my love for learning and doing research in areas that intrigue me. But I also have other strong values: quality time with my wife and children, love for the outdoors, and enthusiasm for other creative endeavors, such as music and movies. Aware of the value each of these holds for me, I can give them high priority and guard against letting them be bumped aside by other activities that may be acceptable, but not as important in my life.

Of course, placing hobbies and avocations high on your list does not mean minimizing the importance and value of work. While everyone's "values filter" is unique, vocation should rank prominently among our priorities. Work is one of life's givens; it is part of everyone's destiny if he or she is to experience a fulfilling, meaningful life. You may dislike your current job, but I have observed again and again that the misery of *not* working is far worse than the misery of working. Even people who don't need to work continue to do so because it provides a sense of accomplishment and purpose. Bill Gates, who reportedly is worth more billions of dollars than you or I can even comprehend, certainly doesn't need to work for a living, but I can't imagine he spends much time contemplating retiring. Work has intrinsic value, whether you are dependent on your next paycheck or not.

For many people who have worked for decades and forged long and productive lives, "retirement" typically does not mean ceasing from work. Instead, even if these individuals have the means to pursue the so-called "good life" of round-the-clock rest and recreation, they don't find it all that appealing. The happiest, most fulfilled "retirees" I know have simply adjusted their careers to fit the latter years of their lives.

I think of my good friend Roger Birkman, the developer of the Birkman Method personal assessment, and my mentor Jim Petersen. Roger, who at this writing is eighty-two, remains very actively involved in his company, although he has turned daily operational responsibilities over to his daughter, Sharon. Nevertheless, he continues to eagerly explore ways that his assessment tool can be used to serve more and more people, particularly in the business and professional worlds.

Jim, who recently turned seventy, has had a long and fruitful career, too, but continues to travel around the world, teaching and mentoring. He also maintains an ambitious schedule for writing significant books on spirituality.

So without question, work should be a part of anyone's values filter. The key, however, is to ensure that it does not become such a priority that it overwhelms everything else. Jobs are important, but I
can't think of any job that would deserve the term *priceless*.

When I finally had the opportunity to devote all my time to my
life's work of mentoring and developing leaders, I became immersed
in it. I loved it so much, in fact, that when I finished for the day I felt
spent, like a sponge that had been wrung dry. I would pull into my
driveway with no emotional stamina or energy remaining for my wife
and children. It was their turn, they rightly expected, but I was empty,
with nothing left to give. Understandably, this created a lot of tension
in our home for a couple of months until I realized the need to make
some adjustments.

I had no doubt that I was engaged in my life's work, but I was
not about to let it detract from my family relationships.
Thankfully, my values filter alerted me of potential danger. So I
resolved to continue working as diligently as possible, but had to
work smarter, being more cautious to avoid making my calendar
too crowded or trying to see too many people. I learned the hard
way to filter everything through my commitments to my family, in
terms of both time and energy. Fortunately, I responded before my
passion created a crisis.

FINDING VALUES THROUGH OUR NEEDS

One of the realities I have learned from personal experience and
through mentoring is that we each have unique needs. A need I
have may not be one that you share, but whatever our needs are,
we must address them or face the consequences of stress and frustration. These needs typically fall into four categories: physical,

emotional, intellectual, and spiritual. Again, what these needs look like specifically will vary from individual to individual, but they are valid and important and should find a prominent place in our values filter.

In my case, I have a need for vigorous exercise. I played sports in high school and college, and have maintained my physical conditioning disciplines to this day. They figure prominently among my values as I recognize how beneficial they are for my long-term health. Even when I have been dealing with heavy work pressures, I have made it a point to work out. If I don't, I can't escape the feeling that something is wrong.

Another need I have is for time alone. Even though I project high energy and a love for people outwardly, inwardly I need time alone to recharge my batteries and to process my thoughts. Particularly at times when I have a number of meetings to attend and need to spend a lot of time with people, I feel under great stress if I don't get adequate time alone.

We all have to be careful when an opportunity comes along that might sound like a good cause to pursue. The fact that these opportunities present themselves (and they will) does not mean we are obligated to accept them. Suppose you are involved in a nonprofit organization, maybe the school PTA or a favorite charity. You learn that there is a vacancy on the board, and someone asks if you would be willing to serve as an officer. If you are inclined to do so and it passes through your values filter, by all means do it. But just because a task needs to be done does not mean you have to be the one to do it. A popular devotional writer, Oswald Chambers, wisely declared many years ago, "A need does not constitute a call." Your values filter can help you to distinguish between the two.

HOW TO ACHIEVE BALANCE WITHOUT HOW-TO'S

I know we live in a how-to world. Many of the most popular books in any retail store are those that purport to boil down any undertaking into a series of simple action steps: "Sell Anything in Three Easy Steps" or "Five Simple Tips for Winning an Olympic Gold Medal." But I have to tell you that there is no single, foolproof method for achieving balance in one's life. No one has been able to explain how to establish priorities so that they never get ignored. But I think the concept of a values filter can be an invaluable help. Here are a few other suggestions:

Examine our own lives and learn how we get out of balance. While we will never be able to achieve and sustain absolute balance, we need to continue striving for it anyway. Remember, no one can teach above where they are living. In addition, if we understand what causes imbalance in our own lives, we will be better able to relate to the struggles of our mentoring partners. We can share from our own experience, proving we aren't perfect (if there was any doubt), and also giving hope to our partners when they wrestle with seemingly insurmountable obstacles. This is an area that I constantly examine in my own life, making sure I hold true to my values for family, physical fitness, mentoring men, spending sufficient time alone, and cultivating my spiritual life.

Help our mentoring partners to think and reflect. Almost without exception, whenever I ask a mentoring partner what is really important to him, he finds it difficult to give me an immediate answer. That's okay. We typically don't go through a day introspectively, wondering, "What is truly important to me?" Most of the time, what seems important at any moment is the urgent matter at hand. So I encourage my partners to go off and give the question some serious consideration.

We have largely lost our ability to think and reflect on important matters. Because most of us have grown up in a world where TV and other media dictate for us what we should think, along with the frantic pace at which we are asked to lead our lives, we tend to err by settling for good things and missing out on the *priceless*.

What is most startling for my mentoring partners, once they have spent some time thinking about what is important for them, is the realization that much of what they do each day has little connection with what they would claim to be most important. This is why I explain to them about this so-called tyranny of the urgent. Urgent matters have an annoying, disconcerting way of crowding out the important — like the squeaky wheel that always gets the grease. In focusing perhaps for the first time on what is really important to them, they may even want to make a list. Items they include may be based on what they have discovered through crisis, passion, and pain. The list does not have to be long, but it can prove to be enlightening for them.

Interact on what they discover. After they have ascertained what they believe is truly important to them, we can then walk with our partners and help them in aligning activities with the priceless aspects of their lives. This may take the form of goal setting. Your mentoring partner may be pleasantly surprised to find how much easier it becomes to set goals once priorities have been clarified.

This interaction also involves helping them determine how to remove obstacles that stand in the way of those things they have recognized as important. As David, a friend and new mentoring partner, recently told me, "Dave, this is how I see you: Everyone has wedges in their lives that keep them from achieving what is most important to them. You help take away the wedges." But remember: As with other stages of the mentoring journey, this usually does not happen instantly; it's a process.

Sometimes work demands make it particularly difficult to keep priorities from being shoved aside. Stan is an attorney I have been mentoring. Because he bills by the hour, time is crucial for him and his typical day does not offer much flexibility. Many people encounter this dilemma. Faced with tremendous demands to produce each day and meet quotas established by his law firm, Stan must live with this tension constantly.

Understanding his priorities, however, helps greatly, because he remains careful to avoid adding more to his load than necessary. His wife and children are very important to him, and he has developed a great passion for mentoring others, so those are the two primary areas he emphasizes. It takes conscious effort, but Stan has succeeded in not neglecting his family — unlike so many people in his profession who deal with similar expectations — and has managed to become extremely effective as an attorney, husband, father, and mentor of others.

Maintain heart-to-heart accountability. Once we have identified what is important and we understand that putting these priorities into action in our lives should not be rushed, we then can establish a true accountability relationship that becomes more and more meaningful for both parties. We want these values to become personal convictions for our mentoring partners, not just more activities to perform. This is why I strongly encourage what I call heart-to-heart accountability. Such accountability is not one-way but two-way. It is not putting high expectations on each other; it involves a continual, two-way dialogue.

This type of interaction can sustain a relationship for a long time. In heart-to-heart accountability there is tremendous mutual benefit for mentor and mentoring partner. The mentor candidly shares the tension he or she experiences in maintaining balance with priorities. The mentoring partner sees the importance of striving for balance, learns that balancing work and personal demands requires lifelong commitment, and enjoys the advantage of having someone to help him or her achieve it.

Mentors serve as models, albeit imperfect ones. We need to demonstrate an awareness of what is most important in our lives and to seek to give those things high priority. Beyond that, we help our mentoring partners to retain the new focus they have for their lives, this new sense of what is important — even priceless — for them.

Accountability can be based on performance, but that is not what we are after in mentoring. Our concern is people, not performance. Therefore, heart-based accountability must be our goal, focusing first on the relationship, regardless of performance.

The most effective leaders and managers I have seen in business understand heart-to-heart accountability. They are concerned about performance but know that if the heart is in the right place, performance eventually will fall in line. Proverbs 23:7 states it this way: "For as he thinks within himself, so he is" (NASB). Genuine, enduring change must start on the inside and work outward.

In addition, because of the trust, credibility, and genuine compassion that has already been established, this kind of accountability relationship provides an open environment for talking about hard issues, the kind that can be shared only in the strictest confidence.

We already have covered a lot of territory, looking at many facets of the mentoring process. But if you were to define the one overriding outcome that a mentoring relationship should have, what would you say it is? I'll give you my answer in the next chapter, but I would like you first to give the following questions some thought.

How Is Your Balancing Act Coming Along?

1. As you have read through this chapter, have you considered what *your* priorities are? What would classify as priceless? If you have not yet done this, take some time to reflect and then tell someone what you have concluded.

2. Once you have clarified what you understand to be your top priorities, be honest: How successfully have you maintained them as priorities?

3. What obstacles might need to be removed if your priorities are to take their rightful place in your life?

4. How do you relate to the concept of having a personal values filter? Would this be helpful for you? Why or why not?

CHAPTER 7

THE SUBSTANCE OF MENTORING

PRINCIPLE #7: EFFECTIVE MENTORS MODEL CHARACTER.

*L*et's suppose, in keeping with our discussions over the last several chapters, you have worked through a variety of issues with your mentoring partner. You have helped your partner to discover how to try to align his or her personal passions with vocation. You have emphasized the importance of formulating a values filter to sift through the varied and often conflicting demands of everyday life to achieve some level of balance. And you have demonstrated the worth of confiding in and comforting partners as they seek to address the various sources of pain and adversity in their lives. Is your mission accomplished? Not by a long shot.

Our purpose in guiding our mentoring partners through the maze of unfulfilled passions, skewed priorities, and ongoing stress is not simply to help them find relief and attain happiness. In fact, relief may be the least important benefit of wrestling through these issues. That's because our focus is not carefree living but the formation of what I like to refer to as "the substance of mentoring": character.

Before we look at why developing character is so crucial to a life-changing mentoring relationship, let me make a comment or two.

Talking about character is tough. In fact, this may be the most difficult chapter in this book. My goal is not only to exhort you, but also to challenge your thinking, just as mine has been challenged over the years. At the very least, if the following discussion of character raises questions in your mind or causes you to reconsider some long-held assumptions, then I will feel this chapter has done its job. When we ask questions, we are demonstrating a willingness to learn, and it never hurts to reexamine our beliefs occasionally and why we hold to them.

One other thing: In this discussion of character and the conclusions I have reached, please don't think I'm saying that I have "arrived" or that I consider myself an accomplished expert on the topic, because like everyone else, I am still a work in process. Hopefully, as we work through this chapter, we'll be learning together.

I'd like to start by asking you a question: What words come to your mind when you hear someone speak about "character," or "personal character"? When I have asked this question in a variety of settings, most people have responded with words like *honesty*, *integrity*, *truthfulness*, or *good ethics*. When I probe deeper for different answers, however, often all I receive is a blank stare. While these terms are safe, stereotypical answers for how we view character, they are just the tip of the iceberg.

Take "good ethics," for example. During my business and professional career, I have met a number of ruthless individuals who practiced good ethics. No one could question their ethical behavior in business matters, but in their relationships with people — coworkers and subordinates, in particular — they are often harsh, uncaring, and manipulative. I used to make sales calls on a guy like that. He was highly competent and exhibited high integrity from a business standpoint, but he was very callous when interacting with people. Because he had a high position of authority, it was not unusual to hear him screaming at other sales reps, and often he caused his own secretaries to cry. What made it worse was that he always displayed a Bible on his desk. Would you describe a person who abuses other people as someone of good character? I wouldn't.

THE CURRENT CRISIS OF CHARACTER

Today, perhaps more than ever, it's important to probe much further into the idea of character. It has become a huge issue in business today in the wake of scandals surrounding once thriving and hugely profitable companies like Enron, WorldCom, Adelphia, and a seemingly increasing number of others. Serious character issues also have been raised at the uppermost levels of government. Highly respected and honored top officials and executives have fallen to disgrace. The circumstances may differ somewhat, but at the heart of this dilemma, weak character deserves much of the blame.

One dictionary defines *character* as "a distinctive trait, quality, or attribute; an individual's pattern of behavior or personality; moral constitution, good reputation, moral strength, self-discipline, fortitude." That covers a lot of ground, but because our concern is how character relates to mentoring, let me suggest a simpler definition: Character is *what is left after the fire*. In other words, it's the proof of who you really are as revealed after being tested and refined by life's experiences, in good times and bad times. Just as bumping a full bucket causes its contents to spill out, a person's character is what spills out when he or she encounters the bumps of life.

You may be wondering what this looks like in a mentoring relationship. To understand this, it's important to go to the very root of character, the foundation that holds good character together. Without question, honesty, integrity, and ethics are important elements of character, and these are qualities we would like to see manifested in the lives of those we mentor. However, the word that best captures what character ultimately means is *humility*. In fact, just as character is the substance of mentoring, I am convinced that humility is the substance of character. Taking it one step further: to be effective mentors we must model character, which means we also must model humility.

Now, *humility* is not a word we often use or even feel comfortable using, is it? In the world of sports and business, where I have spent much of my life, I can't recall hearing the word *humility* come up in casual conversation very often. In fact, years have probably passed without me hearing it used even once. Perhaps that is because many people equate humility with weakness or a lack of strength, courage, and assertiveness. People who are humble according to our stereotype are timid, fearful, and incapable of making sound decisions.

To mask our discomfort with the concept of humility, we have even made it into a punch line for some of our jokes. For instance, have you heard about the service club that awarded a badge of honor to the member exhibiting the most humility, and then took the badge away from him when he wore it? Or maybe you have heard the old country-western song's refrain, "Oh, Lord, it's hard to be humble when you're perfect in every way"?

As I was playing basketball in high school and in college, and when I got my first jobs, humility was not a trait I aspired to cultivate. I wanted to succeed — whatever it took — and I could not imagine how being humble would help. But early in my business career, experiences began to reshape my paradigm of what true humility looks like.

Don VanVolkenburg and I managed a health club in Atlanta after I graduated from San Diego State University. Time after time, I saw Don put my interests ahead of his, even though I was only an employee. He accepted me for who I was and always made himself available to me, no matter what. And it wasn't just me. Over and over I saw Don put others ahead of himself, even if it was inconvenient, simply because he valued our needs and concerns more highly than he did his own.

It's not that Don was just some nice, mild-mannered guy who hated to hurt anyone's feelings. He was strong, confident, and decisive about where he was headed but was not about to run over someone to get there. As the months passed, his consistent selflessness made a strong impact on my life, especially spiritually. Don was the first person to live out for me what I later discovered the Bible teaches in Philippians 2:3-4: "Do nothing out of selfish ambition or vain conceit, but in humility consider others better than yourselves. Each of you should look not only to your own interests, but also to the interests of others."

Sometimes the obstacles confronting us prove too overwhelming, and despite our best efforts, we fail. At times like these, we can discover what a profound, humbling teacher failure can be.

My brother, John, and I had started a construction company. John was a master craftsman, but neither of us knew anything about business. And we were starting up at the worst possible time, during the late '70s and early '80s, when double-digit inflation rates discouraged almost everyone from buying houses. As the new-home market disappeared, we were forced to shift to remodeling existing homes. This kept us going, but it was a weekly struggle trying to make enough money to keep bill collectors at bay and put food on the table.

We landed one job that, once we got paid, would keep us going for another couple of months, but it was trouble from the start. We made an error with some flooring, and even though we apologized and promised to make it right at no additional cost, the customers became irate. It seemed we could do nothing right for this couple, and more than once I was tempted to give them a piece of my mind that I couldn't afford to lose.

Uncertain about what we should do, I discussed the situation with my mentor Dave. To be honest, I was hoping he would suggest that we sue these disagreeable people. Instead, he advised me to humble myself, correct the mistake without saying anything, and tell them that once we had completed the work, they would not have to pay us if they weren't satisfied. As strapped as John and I were financially, these were difficult words to hear, but I followed Dave's advice. We finished the work — feeling it was a top-quality job — and, even though they said they would, the couple never paid us. As you can imagine, that was hard, but because I humbled myself, I harbored no guilt or regrets, and I felt no anger or bitterness, only forgiveness. I had an overwhelming conviction that regardless of the outcome, I had done the right thing. What a painful but powerful lesson in humility, one that was worth far more than any amount the customers could have paid us.

My first experience in seeing humility in a corporate culture came through Dick Rehovit, my sales manager when I first got into the healthcare products industry. Dick was a very dynamic, outgoing man, and I will never forget his words as we sat down together shortly after I had joined the company. He said, "Dave, your job is to get results. My job is to carry your briefcase." In other words, it was his job to make me look good, to help me to succeed. As I look back, it's easy to see that is exactly what he did, not only with me but also with everyone else on the sales team in our region. That's why we consistently remained at or near the top in productivity among the company's sales regions nationwide. Dick's unselfish leadership inspired and motivated us to perform to the maximum.

Years later I saw this principle portrayed on a movie theater screen in another way as I watched *Saving Private Ryan*. If you saw the film, you will remember that four of Private Ryan's brothers had been killed in battles during World War II. Because Ryan was the only surviving son, an executive order had been issued for a team of soldiers to find him and get him home safely. As the story unfolded, it presented an incredible example of what it means to value others above one's self.

In the process of trying to find Ryan, two men in the squad were killed. When the remaining soldiers finally found Ryan, they resented having paid such a high cost to save one man. However, when they discovered that the private was not a coward and that he refused to leave his unit as it faced imminent enemy attack, the soldiers humbled themselves and rallied around him, determined to defend Ryan's unit to the death, which many of them did.

ALL FOR ONE AND ONE FOR ALL

My father was a veteran of World War II and the Korean and Vietnam wars. He once told me that if anything instills humility — the resolve to put others first — it's a great cause. Obviously, war is one of these and so are more common pursuits such as starting and sustaining a business, building a strong family, or developing a championship sports team. When you sense you are engaged in something important, it becomes easier to adopt the motto of the Three Musketeers: "All for one, and one for all."

But it takes more than just a great cause or a catchy motto to instill the foundational character trait of humility. It also requires adversity. The slogan "no pain, no gain" is not just someone's clever idea. But how can we gain from pain? What possible good can come out of the struggles we face in life, whether they occur in the midst of good times or very tough times?

To answer that, we can take a simple lesson from nature. As you probably know, if you cut down a tree and look at a cross-section of its trunk, you will see a series of rings. Each ring represents one year in the life of the tree. The rings, however, are not identical in width. The wider rings indicate years of rapid growth, when weather and other environmental conditions were ideal. Narrower rings, however, show times when growth was difficult, often because of a shortage of rain or other harsh weather. Interestingly, the rings formed during the more stressful years are harder and stronger than the wood that makes up the wider rings.

In a similar manner, the adversities in our lives can strengthen us in a variety of ways. Sometimes they cause us to tap inner resources that we didn't realize we had. They teach us the importance of perseverance as we continue to strive toward our goals. If we let them, the hardships in our lives can build humility. And the fruit of humility is honor, according to Proverbs 18:12: "Before his downfall a man's heart is proud, but humility comes before honor."

Our company had a network of distributors for our product line. As soon as we placed a sale, we would contact the appropriate distributor and arrange for the equipment and supplies to be shipped immediately to the hospital that needed them. One particular day, I contacted a distribution company and placed my order. Instead of filling the order, however, the manager of the company back-ordered the product and it did not arrive as I had promised it would. When vital products such as anesthesia or surgical supplies are not available, it's bad news for everyone involved.

When the order failed to come as expected, the hospital administrator called me on the phone, extremely upset. Upon hearing what had happened, I blamed the problem on the distributor, explaining how I had done everything I was supposed to do. The administrator would have none of it. "Cut the crap. I'm tired of hearing your excuses. *You* dropped the ball. This is *your* fault. I want you to come in with your manager next week," he said, making it clear that we would not be there for a social call.

Before I responded, immediately the words of that proverb on humility came to my mind. I instantly humbled myself and told him, "I will take full responsibility for this problem and I will bring my manager in next week to see you." Even though I knew I was not at fault, I had learned to value the interests of the customer more than my own. But I also knew I had a choice: I could take the way of pride and arrogance, standing on my rights and defending myself from accusations of wrongdoing, or I could go the way of humility. I chose humility.

The following week, my manager and I went to meet with the administrator, whose anger had not abated much. Once again he expressed his view that the fault rested with me and proceeded to tell my manager everything he thought I was doing wrong.

Once he had finished speaking, I looked squarely at the administrator and replied, "Thank you so much for your feedback. I count it a privilege to serve you and your hospital. Because of this, you're going to make me a better sales representative." He looked shocked, but I meant every word of it. In the future I would know better than to presume that the distributor would follow through on critical orders; I would double-check to make sure the orders were expedited properly.

A week later, the administrator called me again. My initial thought was, "Aw, man, now what went wrong?!" But to my shock, he wanted to give me a huge volume of business that normally would have taken months to cultivate. Now it was the people at my company and many peers in my industry who were shocked. "How did you do it?" they wanted to know. I honestly didn't know, other than to see it as proof of the truth that humility comes before honor.

IT TAKES HUMILITY TO PUT OTHERS FIRST

When I spend a day or two with a company's senior executive team, especially one that has expressed a desire to develop their people and become more focused on the customer, I usually ask a couple of open-ended questions to spark their thinking. For instance, at one meeting I inquired, "What would happen if you valued your customers more than yourselves?" One of the executives quickly replied, "Our customers would love it!" Then I asked, "Would valuing your customers more than yourselves have a positive effect on your bottom line?" "Big time," another member answered.

Then I shifted gears a bit: "What would happen if you valued the people who work in your company more than yourselves?" "We would have a lot of happy, loyal, highly motivated and productive people," was the response. "Well, let's go one step further," I suggested. "What would happen if each of you in this room valued each other more than yourself?" One particularly zealous senior executive shouted, "We would be unstoppable as a company. We would take over the world in our industry!" That may have been a bit of an overstatement, but I think he got the point.

That day, as I typically do, I asked the hardest question of all: "What does it really take to value our customer, our people, and our team more than ourselves?" The response is always the same: "We have to serve them." Then I continued, "What does it really take to serve someone else?" No one jumped up with a response. All I saw were vacant stares. After a few uneasy moments, I broke the tension by offering my answer: "We talk about serving, but we don't serve, because it takes great humility. We don't like that term, do we? Do you know why? Because it involves losing our rights — and we love our rights. It involves putting the interest of others over ours, and it begins right here in this room."

I'm not surprised when people don't reach this conclusion on their own. It doesn't fit our grid, and we don't feel comfortable when we hear it. "If we do that, we're going to get run over, taken advantage of," people often reply. They think humility runs counter to being competitive, assertive, determined to accomplish an objective, and other traits typically associated with success in our free-market society. The fact is, however, the best leaders can have those inner drives and also be people of great humility. Rather than weakness, humility at its core is strength, power, and courage — all kept in control and balance, and used for the benefit of others, not for personal gain and advancement.

After teaching this in business seminars and imparting it through coaching and mentoring relationships, Jim Collins wrote an article in *Harvard Business Review* that confirmed what I had discovered through personal experience. Collins, a noted management researcher, and his research teams studied 1,435 companies that had appeared in the FORTUNE 500 from 1965 to 1995. Collins wanted to know what distinguished "good" companies from "great" companies, those that showed consistent, cumulative stock returns well above the general stock market for at least fifteen years in a row. The ones that received the ranking of "great" compiled overall stock returns nearly seven times the general stock market after a key transition point.

What intrigued me were his conclusions about factors that made these companies great. Initially, he instructed his researchers to downplay the impact of top executives to avoid the pitfall of attributing all success — or failure — to the leader. He writes, "Over the course of the study, research teams kept saying, 'We can't ignore the top executives even if we want to. There is something consistently unusual about them.'" This "consistently unusual" appraisal was what they later termed "Level 5 Leadership" — "a paradoxical combination of personal humility and professional will."[1]

Interestingly, most of these level 5 leaders were not the bigger-than-life, charismatic leaders who often star for their companies in TV commercials and appear on the covers of business magazines, but executives who were reserved and gentle, quick to ascribe credit to everyone but themselves, yet who also exhibited great intensity and tenacious resolve.

The most startling fact of Collins' study was that out of the 1,435 FORTUNE 500 companies only eleven qualified as having moved from "good to great" — eleven companies run by level 5 leaders who exhibited humility and fierce resolve. I think this gives us a glimpse of why we have a vacuum of leadership in organizations today.

THE REALITY OF HUMILITY

If you want to know more about Collins' study and his conclusions, you can look up the article or read his book, but the key concept for those of us involved in mentoring is that even in the most successful companies, humility is a desirable quality — maybe even indispensable. What the Collins study showed is that this is not ideology or pie-in-the-sky idealism, but reality. The data from his research was overwhelming. After reading his article, I thought, "Wow, this is what I have been imparting through mentoring and coaching relationships for years. Finally, we have empirical evidence that proves it."

At Leader's Legacy, our motto is, *Developing Great Leaders Who Develop Great Leaders*, and at the heart, this is what we all should be about as mentors. For a mentoring relationship to work, both mentor and partner have to be mutually honest and sincere about their lives. Superficiality won't get it done. However, the greatest test in mentoring is how our partners handle failure — and success. The outcome of both should be humility, and mentors should be able to demonstrate this through example.

Equating humility with failure isn't that difficult. I once heard a radio commentator state that humility is learned through being humiliated, which is commonly the case when we lose a job, find ourselves in serious financial straits, experience trouble in marriage or family relationships, or fall far short of a long-cherished goal. When we suddenly find ourselves in dire situations we cannot control and don't know how to fix, that can be extremely humbling. Failure has a wonderful way of neutralizing our egos and transforming us from doers to learners. We're eager to learn what went wrong and what, if anything, we can do to correct it.

Success is a different matter. Like the athlete or actor who starts believing his or her laudatory press clippings, we can easily become puffed up when things start going well in our lives. If we're not careful, we might break our own arms patting ourselves on the back. Without exception, every person I have mentored who has become successful struggles with humility in the midst of success. That's why I always caution them, "It should humble you more during great times than in tough times, because you can be assured that tough times are right around the corner."

Once again, I have found that the Bible has tremendous wisdom to offer in this area. Proverbs 27:21 states, "The crucible for silver and the furnace for gold, but man is tested by the praise he receives." Isn't that true? People don't feel particularly boastful when the world is collapsing around them. But when good things start happening, do they start feeling proud and impressed with themselves? Adversity shapes character. Success does not develop character, but reveals it.

The great thing about true humility is that in good times and bad times, it enables our egos to remain in neutral. We remain moldable because we remember and understand our inadequacies, and even our mortality. We also have to admit that we really don't have our act together, that we're still learning. As my friend Mark Pollard puts it so well: "A humble man is a wise man. A wise man is a learning man. A learning man seeks to find every lesson in life experiences." This holds true both in good times and tough times.

IS IMAGE EVERYTHING?

In his insightful book *When No One Sees: The Importance of Character in an Age of Image*, philosopher Os Guinness talks about "the modern world's obsession with physical appearance." This came about, he says, when Americans started moving from rural areas to cities, "from small, stable, face-to-face relationships to fast, superficial, largely anonymous acquaintances." This resulted in "an accompanying shift from an emphasis on internal character to one's external appearance. Thus the traditional ideal of 'the strong character' has given way to 'the striking personality' and 'the successful image.'"[2]

We see evidence of what Guinness is talking about every day on billboards, in magazines, in movie theaters, in political races. One familiar TV commercial some years ago made the assertion, "Image Is Everything." But I can't emphasize strongly enough that in mentoring, image is nothing. We are looking to the heart, trying to mine the gold that lies deep within the person we are privileged to mentor.

If we are truly mentoring from the heart and to the heart, we have to get below the surface to what's really going on inside. This includes probing to discern whether our mentoring partner is exhibiting true humility or false humility and being willing to perform the same examination on ourselves. As we all have experienced, outward appearances can be terribly deceiving.

That's why it's important for mentors to model genuine humility in our own lives. Humility is a quality that is more caught than taught. We cannot reproduce in others what does not exist in our own lives. And if we're arrogant and full of ourselves, it won't take long for the mentoring partner to pick that up.

Just as the administrator rebuked me for failing to fulfill my responsibilities, there are times when a mentor needs to impress an important concept on a mentoring partner or even try to give correction when he or she seems off track. At such times, the partner also can respond in one of two ways: pridefully, seeking to defend and justify, or with humility, being willing to seriously consider the wisdom the mentor is offering.

When we evaluate how long to continue mentoring someone, I believe this issue of humility is an important indicator. It's not unusual to find some degree of arrogance in emerging leaders who desire to be mentored. After all, they typically are ambitious and confident, eager to get ahead. They may have many unresolved issues in their lives, but the world has taught them that assertiveness and aggressiveness lead to success. "Look out for number one!" remains the rallying cry for many people today, particularly in the business and professional worlds. The question is, how strong of a foothold does pride have in their lives?

When a mentoring partner displays arrogance in a general way, I try to correct him gently. It's not a matter of wills; I just want to see how the partner responds. If he is teachable, he's willing to seriously consider what I say and respond in a way that shows a desire to learn. If you have a mentoring partner who remains arrogant and clearly seems unteachable, extending the relationship is a waste of time.

Before you start thinking that I wear a badge that reads "Mr. Humility," let me admit that I have a tendency to be arrogant. Maybe that's why I can so easily recognize it in others. I'm very competitive and, being an ex-jock and a sales type of person, I suppose arrogance comes somewhat naturally. But I have discovered the dangers of acting pra pridefully, and whenever someone lets me know that I'm acting in an arrogant way, I try to humble myself immediately. I'm sincerely grateful for people who bring that to my attention, because it's so easy to slip back into old behavior patterns.

So how do you present humility so that mentoring partners will "catch" it? I have found that one of the best ways is simply to share failures as well as successes from your own experiences. Tell about circumstances that humbled you and how you dealt with them. If you handled them poorly, that's fine, because mentors aren't expected to model perfection and it also shows you're human. Our partners need to see examples of humility in action.

A friend of mine, whom I will call Roderick, is a good example. Have you ever seen the book *The Millionaire Next Door?* Roderick is one of those guys. If you judged him by his outward appearance, you would be hard-pressed to perceive him as a very successful business-man. He doesn't live in the best house, will never amaze you with his wardrobe, and certainly makes no effort to draw attention to himself in any way.

Despite being a person of great humility, he's recognized as an E. F. Hutton kind of guy — when Roderick speaks, people listen. He feels very fulfilled professionally, has a tremendous family, and possesses greater wealth than most people would ever dream of having. Yet for years his driving passion has been to invest his life by mentoring other men, showing them the way to find meaningful lives. When he meets with other men, he comes across as quiet and gentle, but the wisdom he imparts has the power of a pile driver — unassuming, yet unforgettable.

A CURE FOR CONFLICT

Humility offers another phenomenal benefit. Have you ever had a conflict with someone — and both of you were right? It could have been someone working with you, your spouse, or a good friend. You find yourself in this intense, interpersonal struggle, both of you taking a stand with no room for compromise. You start pushing at each other verbally, both determined to get your way. Here again there are two options: arrogance or humility.

You can take the path of arrogance and pride, determined to the death to show that you're right. Unfortunately, with this approach no one truly wins and the conflict remains unresolved. And when conflicts go unresolved, relationships become damaged because there's no forgiveness and no opportunity for reconciliation. Or you can follow the route of humility, sticking with the problem and working through it to a satisfactory resolution. When two people humble themselves, valuing each other more than themselves, what disharmony can come out of that?

This is especially true in marriages and family relationships. Because of familiarity and close proximity, conflict is unavoidable, but it need not be destructive. When we humble ourselves with our mates *and* with our children, we're able to forgive and receive forgiveness. In our more than twenty-two years of marriage, Anne and I can recall only one or two times when we went to bed upset with each other. This has been possible for us because of our willingness to humble ourselves instead of insisting on our own rights; our relationship becomes more important than the issue in dispute.

Over the years, I have mentored many men whose marriages were on the rocks. In sharing from my own experience to help them learn and appropriate the principle of humility, it has been thrilling to see many marriages turn completely around. Humility, unlike pride and arrogance, has a wonderfully appealing — and healing — quality to it, whether it is demonstrated in the home, at the workplace, on the ball field, or anywhere else.

This is true in mentoring relationships, too. If we are to impart the principle of humility, it *especially* has to be practiced in those settings. Because of the salesperson in me, I have a tendency to become highly persuasive, sometimes to a fault. There have been times when I unintentionally offended a mentoring partner. When I realized it, my first thought was to justify what I had said or done, but I have learned that the best approach is to respond with humility and apologize, regardless of the fact that no offense was intended.

One morning Floyd, a young twenty-something whom I was mentoring, was coming on far too strongly in expressing his opinion about an important issue we had been discussing. I rebuked him, not only for his attitude but also for the position he had taken. Suddenly, I realized I had hurt him. Even though I felt convinced that Floyd had been out of line, our relationship was far more important than who was right, so a short time later I asked him to forgive me, admitting I had been wrong in how I responded. He accepted my apology and we were free to move on from there.

The interesting thing is that several times since then, I have observed Floyd applying the "humility approach" with men he mentors. We have both learned how we can say dumb things at times, needlessly offending someone, so now we strive to right the wrong as soon as possible. I have never seen a relationship damaged by someone who embraces the principle that "humility comes before honor."

For some people, the idea of valuing other people above themselves may seem revolutionary. After all, this is not the typical message we receive through the media, in many of our institutions of higher learning, or in most workplaces. Yet, as we have seen, without a doubt humility can have practical and even tangible benefits. The question is, how can it be genuine and not contrived? This leads us to the next area of mentoring that I would like you to consider: spirituality. We will explore that topic in the next chapter, but first, please consider the following questions.

Getting Honest About Humility

1. Do you agree that the concept of humility is typically foreign to our Western culture? Explain your answer.

2. Who have you known or worked with that exhibited humility as I have described it: the consistent ability to regard others as more important than oneself?

3. How do you respond to the definition of character: "what's left after the fire"? Can you think of an experience that illustrates this perspective?

4. If you were to rate yourself from 1 to 10 in terms of understanding and practicing humility, where would you fall on the scale? If you feel you need to improve in this area, what steps do you think you should take?

THE FUEL THAT DRIVES THE ENGINE

. . . .

PRINCIPLE #8: EFFECTIVE MENTORS AFFIRM
THE VALUE OF SPIRITUALITY.

. . . .

*T*here are not too many guys like Chad. He was a gifted individual, a highly successful senior executive who came from a family of significant wealth. Unlike many people, who feel trapped in their jobs, he could do virtually anything he wanted. Despite these advantages, he had reached a point in life where he felt dissatisfied, convinced there had to be something more.

During one of our mentoring sessions, Chad looked up with a pained expression and said, "Dave, you know I'm not religious, but I feel like I'm a spiritual person. I want to learn more about spirituality; I think it can provide some answers that I'm looking for. Can you help me?"

He had come to an important realization: Just as you wouldn't play a football game without goal lines or host a banquet without food, you cannot succeed at mentoring the whole person without taking into account the spiritual dimension of the individual's life.

For many years, the topic of spirituality was treated as taboo for casual conversation. "Keep it to yourself" was the prevailing attitude, particularly in the business world. When I started my career in the late '70s, and even into the '80s, I often heard people make a comment like, "Two things we don't talk about around here are religion and politics."

How times have changed. The cover story of the November 1, 1999, *Business Week* was "Religion in the Workplace." Similarly, the July 2001 *FORTUNE* magazine carried the title "God and Business." Other respected periodicals, ranging from the *Wall Street Journal* to *U.S. News & World Report*, also have devoted extensive articles to the growing fascination with spirituality in all areas of life — even in the world of work.

The *Business Week* feature cited Gallup Poll research showing the dramatic change among Americans in their attitudes toward spirituality in just five years. According to the studies, in 1994 only 20 percent of the respondents felt a need to experience spiritual growth. In 1999, a similar study indicated that number had soared to 78 percent.[1] What had once been regarded as "personal" suddenly had been accepted as suitable for the marketplace.

Results of a study published in the August 2002 issue of *Redbook* magazine echo the rising emphasis on spirituality. It asked women, "What do you think is the key to happiness?" Sixty-three percent said *spirituality* ("life is a lot better when I'm feeling at peace"), compared to 21 percent who responded *children* ("Not a day goes by that they don't make me smile"), 13 percent answered *husband* ("He makes me feel good about myself"), and 3 percent indicated *work* ("I'm stimulated by being around creative people").[2]

One's happiness no doubt is influenced by a variety of interrelated factors, but it's clear that people are placing higher importance on spirituality than at any time in recent memory. Although it is not my primary purpose here to explore this phenomenon and its causes, I think it would be worthwhile to consider some of the factors in this shift.

The dramatic and ever-escalating pace of change and uncertainty that we all have experienced since the start of the 1990s. The so-called "good ol' days," when a person could start a career with a large corporation, work hard, and retire forty years later with a gold watch and a comfortable pension suddenly disappeared in the '90s. Business upheaval, which spawned layoffs and massive downsizing, proved that the corporate "gods" that were expected to supply perpetual employment never really existed. At the same time, technological innovations kept the workplace in continual flux, creating another source of stress and uncertainty. As workers wrestled to adapt to one major change, other changes would follow in fast succession, stripping away any semblance of workplace stability.

The globalized economy, another by-product of advanced technology, has revolutionized traditional business practices; the fate of our national economy now intertwines with what transpires in distant lands. Other dramatic changes in the world, such as the tearing down of the Berlin Wall and the dissolution of the Soviet Union, have boggled our minds, especially for those of us who grew up during the Cold War with the daily fear of imminent nuclear attack. Then the events of September 11 put a totally different face on our concept of "imminent attack."

Major change of any kind — good as well as bad — can be extremely unsettling. Like someone adrift in a sailboat during a tropical storm, we want desperately to find a port of stability, a safe place to weigh anchor. Many people have turned to spirituality in hope of finding such refuge.

A growing desire for relationship and "connectedness," spurred in large measure by technology and an increasingly impersonal society. "High-tech" has led to "low-touch." Unparalleled communication innovations have brought about a streamlined but far less relational working environment. As a young businessman, I could never have imagined the impact the Internet, cell phones, and e-mail would have on how we go through a typical day. We find so much information, literally — and instantly — at our fingertips. These new, more efficient forms of communications have sped up the exchange of messages, but often at the cost of commonplace interpersonal graces, such as eye contact, handshakes, and friendly smiles.

As these changes became integrated into everyday activities, workers in traditional office settings suddenly felt alone, as if marooned on corporate islands. And with the advent of home offices, the sense of isolation experienced by those who no longer commuted to "real" offices became even more acute.

Down deep, men and women began to feel a yearning to be connected with others in a way that didn't rely on a cable, keyboard, or cell tower. Again, they surmised that they might find their solutions through some form of spirituality.

An expanding awareness that science and human reasoning have failed to satisfactorily answer some of life's ultimate questions. As quantum physics — the "new science" — gained acceptance toward the close of the twentieth century, support started to erode for the notion that a random "big bang" served as the catalyst that started all things, initiating a vast chain of events that would bring order out of chaos. More and more members of the scientific community began to regard traditional evolutionary theory as little more than an extravagant attempt to exclude God from the human equation.

Science, which for centuries has taken an antagonistic posture toward all things spiritual, today increasingly finds itself making discoveries that affirm the existence of God. Instead of disproving theological views, scientific advancements are pointing to the conclusion that much of life cannot be explained apart from the divine.

Gerald L. Schroeder, a respected MIT-trained, Jewish scientist, makes this point in his book *The Hidden Face of God*. He explains that what we perceive in the physical world as solid matter — the floor we stand on, a skyscraper, even ourselves — is anything but solid. For example, he states that if the nucleus of an atom could be enlarged to four inches, the surrounding electron cloud would be four miles away, with nothing in between but emptiness. If most of what we see as solid matter is indeed empty space, then what force or energy, he wonders, is holding it all together to make it solid?

Schroeder states, "If we can discover that underlying idea [the energy that holds everything together], we will have ascertained not only the basis for that unity that underlies all existence, but more importantly the source of that unity. We will have encountered the hidden face of God."[3] Interestingly, that is the declaration of Colossians 1:16-17: "For by Him all things were created, both in the heavens and on earth, visible and invisible, whether thrones or dominions or rulers or authorities — all things have been created through Him and for Him. He is before all things, *and in Him all things hold together*"(NASB, emphasis added).

SPIRITUALITY VS. RELIGION

It's important to distinguish "spirituality" from "religion." To the average person, religion is often perceived as consisting of buildings, forms, rituals and traditions, rigid dogma, and exclusivity. Spirituality, however, is regarded much differently. It typically is viewed as intensely personal, involving a relationship with God (or some supreme force), others, and even the world around us. Ultimately, *interconnectedness* serves as a good term to express the way many people conceive of spirituality.

Esteemed business periodicals have affirmed this distinction in articles that acknowledge and give their blessing to the role of spirituality in the workplace. William Pollard, chairman of ServiceMaster, Inc., a company that for decades has been guided by spiritually based values, said in the July 9, 2001, *FORTUNE* magazine, "We can't and shouldn't and don't want to drive people to a particular religious belief. But we do want people to ask the fundamental questions. What's driving them? What is this life all about?"[4]

In "A Study of Spirituality in the Workplace," published in the Summer 1999 *MIT Sloan Management Review*, the CEO of a social service organization identified only as John stated it another way: "I believe strongly that religion should not be discussed in the workplace. On the other hand, I believe not only that spirituality can be discussed in such a manner without dividing people, but that its discussion is absolutely key if we are to create and maintain ethical, truly caring organizations."[5]

Again, it's important to remember that the issue here is spirituality, not religion. While I was in college and then very early in my business career, I sampled many forms of both religion and spirituality — trying to reach God, I suppose. I got involved in Transcendental Meditation for a couple of years and investigated other forms of Eastern mysticism, as well as Buddhism and Hinduism. It was only when I encountered the Bible that I found the life-changing experience I had been looking for. What the Bible introduced to me was not religion, but spirituality — the way I could develop an intimate, personal relationship with God. Therefore, my spirituality comes from the Bible, so I will be communicating from that frame of reference.

However, as mentors it's important for us to respect all religions — even when we disagree with their tenets — acknowledging that religious values and traditions have benefited billions of people through the centuries. Why else would they believe so fervently? Personally, I'm so thankful that all people in the United States have the freedom to worship God as they desire. The key is to operate in the context of our own spiritual beliefs.

But when engaged in a spiritual discussion with someone I'm mentoring, I make it clear that my spiritual context is the Bible. My mission is not to promote any specific dogma, ritual, program, or tradition. Rather, I am intensely spiritual and my desire is for my children to grow up to be intensely spiritual as well. We each are discovering how our spirituality — consisting of our beliefs and values — is what sustains us from day to day. It serves as the basis for everything we do.

Verne, an executive in another city who I have been mentoring, comes to mind. When I first met him, he was totally frustrated and discouraged. Despite being extremely successful in his profession, he was feeling great despair. What he needed more than ever was a friend who cared enough simply to listen.

During our first conversation, Verne brought up the subject of religion. Knowing I was from Atlanta, he mentioned that he had lived there for a few years and had become turned off by the "religious people" he had met. After letting him express his views, I told Verne that I feel the same way about religion, but noted that while I'm not a religious person, I am intensely spiritual. I explained about my spirituality coming from the Bible. Then I asked him if he would like to compare what he saw in religion with what the Bible teaches.

About sixty at the time, Verne was amazed at what I had told him. No one had ever said anything like that to him before. As it turned out, he was wide open to discuss spirituality — he just had no interest in religion. Over the weeks that followed, a part of our mentoring sessions consisted of a free-flowing discussion of the Bible. It was amazing to see what a life-changing experience that was for Verne. Since then, he has changed careers, found a new sense of peace in his life and for the first time understands what it means to have a personal relationship with God.

One day he sent me an e-mail to tell me how much this has meant to him. He said, "Paramount for me in this process has been the dawning realization that religion and spirituality are not necessary linked. This is important because our country has plenty of religion, but inadequate spirituality. Once this hurdle has been cleared, using the Bible for life lessons becomes viable, with the words of Jesus taking on new, powerful meaning devoid of dogma."

We all have encountered some individuals who seem to hold no interest in either religion or spirituality, but most people we meet are religious, spiritual, or a blend of the two. Todd and Janet come to my mind as an example of a couple that has embraced a variety of spiritually oriented activities without becoming religious. Todd is a young man I have been mentoring, and he and Janet are very much a part of a local congregation near their home. They see great value in going regularly to a church building where God is specifically discussed, affording the opportunity to meet and enjoy fellowship with like-minded people. They also appreciate the worship traditions and teachings that their church observes. But unlike many religious people I have met, whose involvement is limited to official, church-sponsored activities, Todd and Janet have fully integrated their spirituality into every aspect of their lives, seven days a week. Their "God-awareness" is just as vibrant on Monday morning or Thursday afternoon as it is when they attend a weekend worship service.

Many people find it convenient to compartmentalize their religion, relegating it to perhaps an hour or two a week, typically on a Saturday or Sunday. They go through the motions while failing to reflect any deep, internalized beliefs that govern their outward lives. Spirituality, however, is what I term "the fuel that drives the engine." It prevails twenty-four hours a day, seven days a week, 365 days a year. It provides the motivation, the hope, the impetus for the things we have discussed earlier: pursuing the passions that uniquely define who we are; dealing with the pain of living in a troubled world; embracing the values that help us establish priorities to give us balance and a measure of order for our lives.

INVESTIGATING SPIRITUALITY

We all can appreciate the importance of an individual's physical, emotional, and intellectual well-being. Increasingly, authorities on the workplace are recognizing that because the spiritual resides at the core of our being, it also must be accommodated in an appropriate manner. For example, in an article titled "The Making of a Corporate Athlete," published in *Harvard Business Review*, Jim Loehr and Tony Schwartz ask how top leaders can sustain high performance when faced with ever-increasing pressure and rapid change. The answer, they conclude, is by applying a principle that all world-class athletes understand: "Recovering energy is as important as expending it."

As Loehr and Schwartz point out, this involves not just physical, emotional, and mental capacities, but also spiritual capacity. This they define as "the energy that is unleashed by tapping into one's deepest values and defining a strong sense of purpose. This capacity, we have found, serves as sustenance in the face of adversity and as a powerful source of motivation, focus, determination, and resilience."

This reality leads to my contention that, in mentoring, a commitment to help an individual achieve balance and wholeness in life cannot be fulfilled without acknowledging — and addressing — the spiritual dimension. As Loehr and Schwartz conclude, "When people feel strong and resilient — physically, mentally, emotionally, and spiritually — they perform better, with more passion, for longer. They win, their families win, and the corporations that employ them win."[6]

As I have mentored people over the years, in almost every case the issue of spirituality comes up sooner or later, with a few notable exceptions. When people talk about seeking purpose or meaning in their lives, they are referring to the idea of interconnectedness, the almost subliminal awareness that they are a part of something much bigger than themselves. At the same time, the chaotic times in which we live — ranging from turbulent stock markets to threats of terrorism — are raising deeper questions, such as whether there truly is a God; where they can find hope and comfort to ease their pain and anxiety; or whether there actually is something (or Someone) holding all things together, as Schroeder argues, when everything seems on the verge of ripping apart.

Isn't it curious that even though as a nation we are wealthier than ever, and most of us take for granted the "good life" that our ancestors could never have imagined, so many people remain discontent? From what I have observed, since the early '90s we have been surrounded by perhaps the grandest spiritual awakening the United States has ever known, and yet it is not driven by a particular denomination or religion. It's based on the growing sense that material comforts will never satisfy, that our only true source for hope, peace, comfort, and meaning is spiritual.

Often we are uncomfortable with discussing the spiritual because it's not something we can see and grasp in our hands. But as Schroeder shows in *The Hidden Face of God*, the things we accept as tangible consist largely of the unseen. Scientists talk about protons, neutrons, and electrons, but we barely understand these particles, and no one has literally seen them. The universe, which is even more incomprehensible in its vastness, is another example. We can look up at the sky and see stars, planets, and our moon, but between them is emptiness — nothing but dark space. I believe spirituality provides answers for what is holding it all together.

CONSULT THE ORIGINAL SOURCES

For this reason, I have never hesitated to discuss spirituality when the subject arises. In fact, I make a point of encouraging the men I mentor to investigate spirituality, whatever it means to them. However, I strongly urge them not to get their information secondhand. Telling them what I learned through my own spiritual quest, I emphasize that to get an accurate view of spirituality you need to go to the original sources, to examine them for yourself. I think of the ancient Bereans, whom the Bible describes in Acts 17:11 as "of more noble character than the Thessalonians, for they received the message with great eagerness and examined the Scriptures every day to see if what Paul said was true."

Of course, for me that means examining the Bible. I believe that if anyone wants to engage in a spiritual discussion, the Bible should be one of the sources considered, but I don't try to force my spirituality on anyone. That approach turned me off during my early days as a spiritual seeker, and I refuse to do that to someone else. I'm a strong advocate for demonstrating mutual respect for each other's views.

At the same time, being true to who we are, I believe we have an obligation to express honestly what we believe spiritually. That's why I'm not at all reluctant to admit that my spiritual quest has led to my becoming a follower of Jesus. Because of what I have learned about him in the Bible — and how that has changed my life, my family, and the lives of many other people I know — I encourage mentoring partners to take an honest look at him for themselves. In sales, when you find something that works, you want to recommend it to others; I believe the same principle applies to spirituality.

Much of the spiritual heritage of the United States is rooted in the Bible. This is one reason I encourage people to take an open-minded look at it. Remember the Kellogg's commercial that suggested, "Try it again for the first time"? When a mentoring partner expresses an interest in exploring spirituality, it would be a disservice not to suggest that he or she consider the Bible, comparing it to any other original sources he or she wants to investigate.

I urge my mentoring partners to be like the Bereans, not accepting the word of other people on spiritual issues without checking it out for themselves. For instance, I find many people intrigued by Jesus Christ, but in plain fact they don't know much about him. Often their perceptions are skewed because they have been formed from someone else's opinion or interpretation. That's why I encourage partners to investigate the actual source of any spirituality, not someone's pre-chewed, already processed view of it. The original sources of any religion, I have found, will speak for themselves and defend themselves — to the degree that they can.

Years ago I was leading a group of young adults in a discussion of spirituality. In response to my opening question, "Are you religious, or are you spiritual?" they each expressed a strong resistance to anything they perceived as being religious. One woman even commented, "If anyone talks to me about religion, I'll smack them in the face, tell them where to go, and walk out. But spiritually, I don't know who the heck is driving the bus up there, but I know someone is."

Weeks later, after participating in our discussion of the book of John, this same woman spoke with tears in her eyes: "I can't believe what I'm seeing. This guy Jesus is so incredible. Dave, why is it that no one has told us about this Jesus before? I have heard all kinds of other things, but no one ever told us about this guy." As time went on, this woman marveled at how significant the Bible became for her.

As I said, people are curious about Jesus; they just don't know much about him, and often what they have heard is inaccurate. If mentoring partners are interested in exploring another religion on their own, I simply recommend that they be certain to study the original source — such as the Torah or the Koran — not a book about the religion or someone's explanation of it. Always let the source speak for itself and the partner will arrive at his or her own conclusions as to whether it seems credible.

One thing I do tell them about Jesus is that he is a much cooler guy than they might think, in part because he also was somewhat turned off by religion and religious people. The key is that the mentoring partner must drive the discussion. This is not the mentor's job, because we are there simply to help the partner in dealing with issues, concerns, and needs in his or her own life. As mentors, we need to be sensitive to our partner's agenda.

Occasionally, this will mean that the spiritual dimension, by the mentoring partner's choice, is not addressed. Gus is a good example. When I met him through a mutual friend, Gus was looking for someone to mentor him, to coach him through some difficult career issues. He was enduring a great deal of stress in his life, and I began meeting with him, talking about his areas of passion, pain, and priorities, and urging him to start looking at some things from a different angle. He was extremely appreciative and began acting on some of my suggestions.

One morning the subject of spirituality came up and we talked about it for a while. Gus seemed very interested, so I asked if he would be open to taking an honest look at the Bible. He said that he was, but after a meeting or two, Gus lost interest and did not want to discuss that area any further. So I dropped the subject and it has not come up again, though I'll be happy to discuss it if he changes his mind.

Gus and I have continued to meet, but we just talk about topics of interest to him, and so far he has not brought up spirituality again. That's okay. I still value his friendship. Although we may believe that to neglect the spiritual side is to shortchange oneself, the partner must set the agenda. The truth is, even if we tried to force our beliefs on our mentoring partners, it would do no good. Partners will only learn what they value and consider important. If they lack interest, no amount of persuasion will change that. An old saying reminds us, "One persuaded against his will remains of the same opinion still."

As I said, Gus is an exception. Most people I meet have an innate spiritual sensitivity. They are curious; they want answers, but they just don't know where to look for them.

Gregg is another man I met through a friend, someone I had mentored in the past. To look at him, you would have thought he had his life sailing along smoothly on exactly the right course. As we talked over lunch, however, I learned his happy, easygoing exterior covered up the internal pain of career indecision, broken relationships, and general frustration about life. Gregg told me he had not enjoyed any of the jobs he had since college, he felt miserable, and he could make no sense out of his life.

I took an immediate interest in this young man, discerning that despite his personal anguish, he had great potential. I told him I would love to mentor him and thought I could help him find the right place in his career. I added that if he had other areas of adversity, I might be able to offer some suggestions. As we were talking, I casually asked, "Are you into religion, or spirituality, or anything like that?" Greg quickly responded, "I'm not religious at all, but I'm very spiritual." I told him that I was much the same, again explaining how I base my spirituality on the Bible. Then I raised a completely unrelated question — something about how he defined the priorities in his life — and the conversation shifted away from spirituality.

We got together the next week and spent most of the time talking more deeply about his career issues. When we were about to leave, however, Gregg looked at me and said, "You know, Dave, when we met last time you mentioned spirituality. I know something is missing in my life, and I think that's it. I don't know if you can spare the time, but if you can, I would love to take a look at the Bible with you, to see if that might help." I told him I would be glad to, and discussions about spirituality and the Bible became an integral part of our mentoring sessions over the next weeks and months.

I slowly saw Gregg's career — and entire life — change dramatically as he took the principles from the Bible to heart and started applying them in different ways. It has taken time, and there have been some serious bumps along the way for him, but it has been so rewarding for me to help him work through life's issues using a spiritual grid. Talking with a mentoring partner about the physical, mental, and emotional aspects of life is fun, but there is something about digging into the spiritual dimension that deepens the relationship more than anything else.

Cultivating a growing relationship with God does not happen overnight, any more than building a successful, loving marriage can be done instantaneously. Both require time and a lot of hard work and commitment. I think of when I first met Anne. She just wowed me, and almost immediately I started thinking that I might want to marry her — but I don't think she was nearly so sure about me. That was more than twenty years ago, and although we have a relationship today that is far better than I could have ever hoped, we are still getting to know each other. The same holds true for mentoring partners seeking to establish an enduring relationship with God. As they see how spirituality can become their foundation, their source for hope, guidance, comfort, and truth — whether the issues are work-related, family-related, or whatever — they discover that the relationship becomes more than they would have imagined.

I could list numerous other examples in which, somewhere between the first and fourth meetings, new mentoring partners initiated spiritual discussions, recognizing that this area of their lives also needed attention. Thinking about it over the years, I have concluded that God has created an insatiable desire inside us. One translation of a statement by French scientist and philosopher Blaise Pascal describes it as "a God-shaped hole (or vacuum) that only God can fill." At the same time, for the mentoring partner spirituality has to make sense; it must be relevant to his or her life. This is why it is so critical to go directly to the original source in a spiritual search. This neutralizes everything else and allows the partner simply to take an honest look and evaluate without having to wade through traditions imposed by people.

For this reason, I always strive for free exchange in conversation. I steer away from injecting my opinion unless it's requested. However, when I first talk with mentoring partners about spirituality, it's common for them to ask how spirituality has impacted me. This becomes another opportunity to let them into my world by explaining how the Bible's teachings changed my life. In particular, I tell about how my relationship with God transformed my relationship with my dad, as well as what it has meant in showing me how to become a better worker, husband, father, and friend.

Sharing personal experiences like this has helped mentoring partners discover that the Bible is not some ancient book without value or application for living in the twenty-first century.

Even though the Bible has become the most powerful, life-changing book I have ever read, I don't want to persuade people to believe it based on my experiences. If the mentoring partner arrives at the same spiritual conclusion, I want him to reach it on his own because he believes it. However, if he loses interest in discussing spirituality or arrives at a different conclusion, the relationship can continue, provided it's not based on the mentoring partner agreeing with the mentor. The mentor's desire should still be to help the partner as much as possible. If you approach the mentoring relationship with the assumption that the partner must become aligned with your own spiritual beliefs, the relationship may be doomed to failure. Although my desire is to see partners value the Bible, I won't force it on them.

HOW TO GET STARTED?

Hopefully, you can now more fully appreciate the importance of helping a mentoring partner examine the spiritual aspect of life. If you are interested in getting started with a spiritual discussion, here are some suggestions that have worked for me with someone interested in looking at the Bible.

Don't use study guides. "Are there any outlines or study guides I can use?" Truthfully, I don't like using study books initially because they are too biased; they have a goal or end result in mind, and the mentoring partner recognizes that. As I have said earlier, it's critical for the partner to examine the original source material, not someone else's interpretation of it. Using study guides often makes the mentoring relationship content-centered and not learner-centered. If we use guides, we may put too much emphasis on the program and can lose sight of the person. I find using the Bible by itself puts us both on equal terms because we are learning together.

Look at yourself first. An important principle in mentoring is to have your own spiritual life in order. As in any other area, you cannot mentor beyond where you are yourself. You can't help someone establish a healthy, personal relationship with God if you don't have that yourself. This does not require that you have "arrived." In fact, the people who believe they have arrived can be assured they have not. The spiritual life is a journey that extends for a lifetime, but we at least need to be headed in the right direction.

The truth is, I have often found that as the mentor, I have bene-fited as much as (sometimes even more than) the mentoring partner from taking part in an honest, open-ended, no-agenda spiritual dis-cussion. It's definitely a win-win for both mentor and partner.

Use the same "Book" for your discussions. If you decide to use a Bible for discussions when your partner raises some spiritual issues, I sug-gest that both you and your partner get the same easy-to-understand modern translation, to avoid confusion. There are so many transla-tions available today, it helps to use the same one so you can discuss the same wording. I have found that the New Living Translation published by Tyndale House and The Message, a very insightful par-aphrase published by NavPress, are the two easiest when starting out.

You can begin by reading either Genesis in the Old Testament or the gospel of John in the New Testament. Both of these books pres-ent foundational spiritual principles that recur throughout the Bible. Sometimes, if a person has a religious background and already has some familiarity with the Bible, I have found it good to read and dis-cuss the book of Romans together, especially chapters 5 through 8.

Whichever book you use, make sure your purpose of offering the mentoring partner an opportunity to take an honest look at genuine spirituality remains foremost in your mind. When mentoring about career or family issues, we can make observations or offer sugges-tions, but we don't tell the partner what to do. The same approach should be taken in addressing spiritual issues. We should be willing to readily share insights from our own experience, but mentoring partners must arrive at conclusions on their own.

Ask open-ended questions. By all means, avoid asking questions that can be answered "yes" or "no." We want to challenge mentoring partners' thinking by letting them discover insights themselves. For this reason, questions that ask what, why, and how are particularly effective. You might pose questions like:

How would you summarize what we just read?
What stood out to you?
Why do you think this (what we read or are discussing) is significant?
What questions does this raise for you?

There are many other ways you can ask probing questions that encourage the mentoring partner to give serious thought to what he or she is studying. Just avoid asking questions that seem to have only one correct answer. We want to know what they are thinking and how they are responding to what they read, and to help them understand that in the process of discovery, there is no such thing as a wrong answer.

Don't force your opinions. We are not asking mentoring partners to believe the Bible (or any other source) or our opinions about it. Our purpose is simply to encourage them to take an honest look at it to see if it offers anything of value to them for everyday living. In most cases, I have found that the mentoring partner gets a lot of positive benefit from the Bible, but if he does not and decides to quit at any time, that is okay. Usually, after he has expressed his view, he will ask what I think, but even then I respond in a way that does not try to influence what he thinks or concludes. My faith in Jesus, for instance, has had a phenomenal effect on my life, but there is no point in trying to force my beliefs on others. For faith to become real for them, they must embrace it on their own.

An accurate perspective on mentoring and the difference we can make as we engage in it requires a long-range view, thinking not only of the immediate but also many years into the future. In the next chapter, we will look at what kind of legacy you will leave behind when your life is over and how involvement in mentoring can shape that legacy. Before you go there, however, I would like you to give some thought to the following questions.

Spotlight on Spirituality

1. Would you describe yourself as religious? Or spiritual? Or both? Explain your response.

2. Do you agree with the distinctions I have made between religion and spirituality? Why or why not?

3. Have you experienced or observed an increase in interest in spirituality among the people you know? If so, how have they expressed this?

4. How do you feel about helping a mentoring partner to address the spiritual dimension of life? Do you have any misgivings about this part of the mentoring package? Why?

THE VISION GAP: FOCUSING ON THE FUTURE

PRINCIPLE #9: EFFECTIVE MENTORS RECOGNIZE THAT
MENTORING + REPRODUCTION = LEGACY.

. . . .

*W*hat will you be doing one hundred years from now? You're probably thinking something like, *Well, nothing, because a hundred years from now I'll be dead.* Then let me ask it another way: What will be the impact of your life one hundred years from now. What kind of legacy will you leave behind?

Does that question stir your thinking? It had that effect on the executive team of an organization I was meeting with some months ago. When I suggested that they discuss some of the major challenges they were facing, one of the leaders commented that the company's biggest problem was that they had no vision. "We need a vision for the next five years," he said. So I inquired what they would like to accomplish in the next five years and began to list their responses on a flip chart. After they listed about five or six items, I said, "These are great goals and objectives, but that's not vision."

Next I asked them what they would like to accomplish through their organization over the next twenty-five years. "Whoa, that's big!"

one executive commented. After some thought, they again started compiling a list. After their list had grown to about five or six items, I pointed out to them, "Do you notice that these items are the same goals you listed in your five-year vision, only bigger and more ambitious? This isn't vision."

Finally, I posed the third question: "What would you like to see accomplished through your company a hundred years from now?" They all sat back with puzzled looks and took a collective deep breath, while some of them scratched their heads. After a minute or two, one of the executives responded, "Well, none of us will be around by then, but we still would like to think that what we're doing today will be having some kind of positive impact."

"Exactly!" I replied. "Now you're starting to think like visionaries. What would that look like?"

Being realistic, they knew their organization probably would not exist in one hundred years, at least not in any form they could readily recognize. It also was highly unlikely that even the building where we met that day would still be standing. So they began to see that a hundred-year vision would have to involve a lot more than bricks and mortar or organizational structures and goals. It would have to boil down to the impact on people: their employees, their customers and suppliers, their families, and others who had some relationship with their company. Suddenly, the conversation about vision took on an entirely different slant.

These executives had just had an "aha!" experience, a moment of unexpected insight that could affect dramatically the way they conducted business — as well as their individual lives. We agreed this involved recognizing that what is achieved in the workplace goes far beyond the numbers on a profit-and-loss statement or the strategy for rolling out a new product. Our conclusion was that the real bottom line of what we do in business, our homes, and our communities is whether we have made a positive difference in the lives of people around us.

Just as vision is essential for organizations, it is equally important for individuals. This is what brings focus to our lives. It also gives us direction, a sense of where we are headed. In his book *Leading Change*, John P. Kotter says vision "motivates people to take action in the right direction. . . . With clarity of direction, the inability to make decisions disappears."[1] As with the formation of a corporate vision, the unique vision we develop for our personal lives needs to be distinguished from goals, although goals can serve an important role in seeing our vision become reality.

At its essence, vision is a mental picture, a perception acquired through life experiences that says to our hearts, "This is what I want to give my life to." It flows out of who we are — our passions, desires, and interests, our values and strengths. Perhaps the hardest thing about vision is shaping it for the long term. Too often our vision does not extend much beyond tomorrow, or next week, or next year. It's good to want to have a positive impact through our lives every day, but I am convinced that a vision worth having is one that should outlive us. I am convinced that my life should have an even greater impact after I'm gone than it has while I'm on earth.

So how does vision relate to the process of mentoring an individual? Is it simply a matter of investing enough time and energy in the life of another person until you see positive changes taking root?

One morning I was meeting with a young executive who has a great heart for mentoring his employees. "What is the goal of mentoring?" I asked him. Without blinking an eye, he responded,

"Character." I was pleased to hear him say that, because as we discussed earlier, character should be a major area of emphasis. We want the people we mentor to become men and women of character. But if we stop there, our vision is too narrow.

Although character is a major goal in mentoring, the ultimate goal of mentoring is reproduction: seeing the people we mentor begin to reproduce themselves by mentoring others. As we invest in our mentoring partners, they learn how to invest in others as well. In that way, the impact we have on our mentoring partners starts to multiply. Over time, that impact can grow exponentially, touching the lives of more people than we could ever imagine.

A few years ago, I was spending a day with my mentor Jim. I knew that because he travels so widely outside the United States, he rarely takes business trips within the country. But as we were discussing our upcoming schedules, he mentioned planning to fly to Minneapolis the next week. "Minneapolis?" I asked. "What in the world are you going there for?"

"That's where my mentor lives," he answered. Jim was in his late fifties at the time and I just stared at him in amazement and asked, "You have a mentor?" He replied, "Why, are you surprised? We all need mentors." I just had to ask another question: "Does your mentor have a mentor?" "He sure does," Jim said, teaching me another valuable lesson: No matter how far along we progress in life, an effective mentor is one who continues to grow and keeps learning. But another reality occurred to me at the same time: I was at least the fourth generation in this mentoring chain, counting Jim, his mentor, and his mentor's mentor. Indirectly, two men I've never met have made a positive impact on my life.

It's important to capture the magnitude of what can happen

when a mentor invests time in people who mentor others, who mentor others, who mentor others, and so on. It's a multigenerational impact, one that can go on indefinitely — long after your time on earth has ended.

This multigenerational impact is what I like to term *reproduction*. Obviously, my own mentoring series did not start with Jim's mentor's mentor and will not end with the man who is mentored by a man I mentor. So when you mentor even one person, who learns how to mentor someone else, what is the potential impact of your life? I can think of only one word to describe it: *limitless*.

At this point, I need to introduce one more term into this discussion. We are no longer talking about mentoring just one individual or showing the way to a better, more fulfilling life; and the point of reproduction is not to accumulate numbers. The bottom line of what we're talking about can be summed up in a single word: *legacy*. Your legacy is the lasting, enduring impact that your life will have long after the black type in your obituary has faded.

In an article explaining how top business leaders and professionals are attempting to restore order to their fast-paced, chaotic lives, *Fast Company* magazine offers this wonderful observation: "If there is one question that's guaranteed to inspire a sense of purpose and discipline, it is — what do you want your legacy to be?"[2] Older men I talk with, guys who have been through the wars of the business and professional worlds as well as in their own lives, often express similar sentiments. These men recognize that they probably have more time behind them than what remains ahead for them. As they see their lives beginning to wind to a conclusion, they desperately want to be assured of leaving an impact, to know their lives will have made a difference in some productive manner. Perhaps for the first time, they sense a need for a commanding focus, a "call" to something truly significant that is much bigger than themselves.

I'm convinced that there is no more effective or more gratifying way for anyone to build a lasting legacy than through mentoring. As acclaimed leadership expert Max DePree says, "Each of us is capable of being a mentor in one way or another. If we think about leaving a legacy, we will establish these relationships, because mentoring is a really crucial element to growth. A million mentors wouldn't be too many!"[3]

Of course, legacies can be established in ways other than mentoring. We think of inventors like Thomas Edison, Alexander Graham Bell, and the Wright brothers. Their ingenuity and imagination continue to leave their mark on humanity today. Scientists like Leonardo da Vinci, Albert Einstein, Jonas Salk, and Madame Marie Curie also have had lasting impacts in the lives of men, women, and children through their discoveries.

We can think of artists, composers, writers, philosophers, and others who have made positive contributions to the world around them that have endured long after they have drawn their last breath. Without question, the founding fathers of the United States left an incredible legacy with their vision of a nation of liberty and opportunity. And men and women like Susan B. Anthony, Martin Luther King Jr., and Rosa Parks left their indelible marks in the quest for equal rights that transcend gender, race, and ethnicity.

However, most of us will never conceive of an innovation that will revolutionize communications or transportation, discover the miracle cure for a dreaded disease, or compose a symphony that will be performed for centuries around the world. It's also unlikely that we will find ourselves in a position to take a landmark stand against bigotry. That does not mean, however, that we cannot establish legacies worth living for — and worth dying for. Through mentoring we can share in the common thread that ties together the giants of history. We can have a profound, life-enhancing impact on the lives of people we encounter from day to day, helping them to improve and strengthen relationships with people in their own lives.

And who knows, maybe someone you mentor directly or someone down your mentoring chain will become that person who finds a life-saving cure, or rises to become a great statesman, or writes powerful words that will continue to pierce the hearts and minds of readers for years and years.

One way to grasp what your impact could look like one hundred years from now is to think in terms of your own family. You may already have children, even grandchildren, but for a moment try to project a hundred years down the road and imagine what could be. How would you like to envision your descendants? While you may not be able to even guess what jobs or pastimes they might have, you can think of the kind of people you would like for them to become. It comes down to values and relationships, doesn't it?

In linking together the ideas of mentoring, reproduction, and legacy, I find grandparenting serves as a helpful analogy. Over the course of this book, I have drawn from my experiences as a parent to show some of the parallels with mentoring. While I can't tell you what it's like to be a grandparent yet, I understand that in some ways it can be even more rewarding than being a parent. Friends have told me that nothing compares with having grandchildren. I'm sure there are many reasons for this, but one of them certainly is the joy of seeing their physical legacies being extended to another generation.

You may have seen the TV commercials featuring William Clay

Ford Jr., chairman and CEO of the Ford Motor Company. These ads point to the dual legacy of Henry Ford, who invented the automobile more than one hundred years ago and literally set the wheels of the automotive industry in motion. But they also tell us that Bill Ford is a fourth-generation Ford at the helm of one of America's leading automotive manufacturers. That is quite a legacy, one that I imagine would make Henry Ford extremely proud. He had a vision for a new way for people to get from one place to another, and now his great-grandson is protecting that vision and passing it on to yet another generation.

The idea of seeing the mentoring process passed on to third, fourth, and perhaps subsequent generations thrills me. It is a privilege and a source of great joy to invest your life in other people as a mentor and watch their lives begin to change for the better. But the joy is even greater when you begin to see — as I have — the people you have mentored begin to mentor others. When that happens, you know that the impact you have had in the life of someone else is beginning to multiply in the life of yet another person.

That's why the principle at the start of this chapter is, *Effective mentors recognize that Mentoring + Reproduction = Legacy.* The investment of our life in just one other person can pay dividends that span decades, even centuries.

Edward was only twenty-seven when I started to mentor him seven years ago. Today he is the CEO of a growing company with more than one hundred employees. The demands on his time are tremendous, especially because he also has a young family. After a full day at work — when he is not traveling for business — it would be understandable if all he wanted to do was drive home and spend the rest of the day with his wife and children. But Edward still finds time to mentor people, building into the lives of others as I did with him. As a matter of fact, it has become a part of his lifestyle. Still a long way from his peak years as a business executive, he already is thinking *legacy*, recognizing that the impact of his life will be measured primarily by the influence he has had in the lives of people who crossed his path.

I think of another young executive who has grabbed hold of the mentoring vision and has already started running with it. Two years ago, when Brian was twenty-three, he recognized the need for a mentor. Even though his career was doing reasonably well, it had failed to meet his expectations after he graduated from college, and his day-to-day struggles were greater than expected. He started meeting with Mark, a man I had been mentoring. I always enjoy meeting with some of my mentoring "grandchildren," so several months later, Brian and I met. I was curious about how his life was progressing.

After Brian had given me a brief overview, I asked him, "Is your *real* vision one of making more money, closing more sales, and becoming a top executive?" There is nothing inherently wrong with any of those, I assured him, but I wanted him to start looking far beyond himself. We talked about building a legacy even at his young age, and I challenged him to think one hundred years into the future and to consider the long-term impact of his life.

Recently Mark, Brian, and I had breakfast together, reminiscing over what had gone on in our lives over the past couple of years. What Brian had to say amazed me, showing a maturity and focus far beyond that of most of his peers. Having realized that there is always another dollar to be earned, another sale to finalize, and another promotion to receive, Brian didn't take long to articulate the vision he had for his life. Soon he responded, "Dave, it all has to boil down to people; I want to have an impact in the lives of people. I know that will be my ultimate legacy, not how much money I made or the titles

I held. I see my work as the way of achieving that, of influencing people in such a way that they will have a better life — and in turn have an impact on others."

Mentoring others would be a key element of this, along with conducting himself in business in a way that would affirm Brian's bedrock values and support the people-centered legacy he hoped to establish. Peers and friends are already being drawn to his character and focus. And I would not doubt that by the time you read this Brian has begun mentoring someone.

When we talk in terms of legacy, we typically think of older people who have lived out most of their lives and now are starting to evaluate what will be the sum total of what they have done. But this idea of establishing an enduring legacy is not something reserved for the twilight years of life. Even people right out of college can get engaged in the mentoring process by working with teenagers, and young business-people can mentor college students. If we can start planting a long-term vision of starting to establish a legacy even in the early years of adulthood, we can help them to become more effective than ever.

One of the greatest weaknesses of emerging leaders, as with most people, is that they don't understand who they really are — their strengths, interests, needs, and values. Vision with an eye toward legacy can give them direction in life. By helping them as mentoring partners to understand their passion, pain, and priorities, we can give them a head start in making a real, long-term difference in the world around them.

Young, old, or somewhere in between — age is not an issue in mentoring. The sooner you get started the better, regardless of whether you are in the opening stages of your adult and vocational life or in the twilight of your career.

INTRODUCING THE IDEA EARLY ON

Whenever I mentor someone, early on I ask the question, "Is this something you think you would like to do someday?" Having already experienced how mentoring has helped them, without exception they respond that they would like to be able to do that with others. Then they often add, "But I don't know how." I assure them that over time, they will learn the how-to's. My purpose in raising the question is simply to stimulate their "want-to."

Several months ago I began mentoring Ray, a CEO in his fifties, and we had a lot of fun working through some critical issues in his business and his life. Having seen firsthand the value of investing in another man, within just six months he began meeting with others at his company and mentoring them. This has paid great dividends for his business, and Ray has found it very fulfilling to draw from his accumulated experience and wisdom to help others who are not as far down life's road as he is.

Now Ray is thinking in terms of legacy. He has grasped the idea that making a lasting commitment to becoming a mentor requires a willingness to look far ahead — one hundred years, not just ten or twenty — and he is running with it at full speed. Like the pebble that strikes the water, starting a ripple that radiates outward long after any evidence of the initial impact has disappeared, he wants the impact of his life to radiate wider and wider, long after his name has faded from most memories.

Keep in mind that there are no guarantees someone you have mentored will mentor someone else. But if you plant the seed in their minds and impart a vision for how they could be used to enhance the life of someone else, more often than not you will eventually see a "sprout." As I learned in sales, there is nothing more effective than a satisfied customer, and in many cases, once people have experienced the benefits of mentoring, they readily understand the value of helping others.

First and foremost, the mentor's own vision must be clear. Ideally, we should proceed as Stephen Covey suggests in his book *The 7 Habits of Highly Effective People:* "Begin with the end in mind."[4] We need to start with a vision for what we would like to see happen a hundred years in the future and work backward. If our desire is to establish a positive legacy that will extend into the next century, we need to focus on the values and principles we wish to impart — and start doing it. That's why it is so valuable to instill the vision for mentoring early on in people's careers. If they embrace that concept, as Brian has, they can incorporate it into their values filters to avoid becoming ensnared by seemingly good pursuits that cause them to veer far from their ultimate goal.

Vision stretches people, challenging them to extend far outside their comfort zones and to grow, even as they are striving to have an impact on others. "Where there is no vision, the people perish," states Proverbs 29:18 (KJV).

At the same time, people want to be developed. Down deep they sense a need for someone who will listen, share from their own experiences, and point them in the direction they want to go. Combine people's need to be developed with the equally valid need to be involved in a mission that is bigger than themselves and you have a great rationale for the mentoring process that addresses the whole person, working from — and to — the heart.

Hear it, see it, do it, reproduce it. This business model I learned years ago applies in sales, management, and many other business pursuits, but it also fits well for mentoring. Through Dave Hill and then Jim Petersen, I heard and saw mentoring principles in action. Recognizing the value it had in my life and desiring to have that kind of impact in someone else's life, I started doing it — with some notable failures along the way, especially at the beginning. With some practice, along with the good old trial-and-error method of learning, I became better at mentoring. In time, the relationships I had established with my mentoring partners were worth reproducing and I started to encourage them to do the same with others.

WHAT ABOUT YOU?

Let me ask you: What are you giving your life to today? And what will be the net result?

Are you striving to build the next great company? Well, remember that businesses come and go. Think of some of the prominent companies of decades past — Montgomery Ward, Kresge & Company, American Motors, and many others — that have faded from the American scene. Even companies that remain usually undergo dramatic change. Take the 3M Corporation, for example. Its name used to stand for Minnesota Mining & Manufacturing, but I don't think they do much mining anymore. Think of other "alphabet" companies, such as AT&T, IBM, and NCR. They are vastly different from the companies they once were.

In this regard, I think of Gordon, the CEO of an organization I consulted with a number of years ago. He was a driver, a classic type-A personality determined to build a company that unquestionably would bear his mark. The business thrived and because he was the key player, Gordon received much of the credit.

One day, however, a serious illness forced him to resign and turn over his leadership responsibilities to someone else. Within months this company, which had become so intertwined with Gordon's persona, style, and skills, collapsed like the proverbial house of cards. Rather than leaving a business legacy, his ineptness as a leader in having failed to mentor and develop other leaders reduced the company to a mere statistic among corporate failures in his city that year.

I remember reading the autobiography of a famous athlete whom I had admired, a man who was idolized by millions of sports fans during his heyday. I don't think I have ever read a more depressing book. In his sixties at the time he wrote the book, this man could do nothing more than reminisce about his sports career. Obviously, his entire identity had become enmeshed with his celebrity and statistics, and it seemed as if nothing good had happened in his life since he retired. Today, many young athletes have no idea who this superstar was. Is this the kind of legacy you would like to leave?

We live in a society that is infatuated with celebrity. In fact, as I once heard philosopher Os Guinness comment, "Some people today are famous for being famous." Singing stars rise suddenly and then disappear almost as quickly; movie stars make a splash and then sink out of sight; star athletes set records one year and appear on waiver lists the next. Recent phenomena are the superstar CEOs who become the focus of magazine ads and TV commercials. But as recent history has taught us, many of these celebrities are not all that "super." In fact, I have a friend who makes it a personal policy not to invest in companies that are led by someone who has become a household name.

When all is said and done, mentors will be among those who have truly made the greatest difference in the lives of people. In a real sense, mentoring is leadership — leading a mentoring partner to self-discovery, self-fulfillment, and paradoxically, selflessness. The words of ancient Chinese philosopher Lao-Tzu apply here: "But as for the best leaders, the people hardly notice their existence, the next best the people honor and praise, the next the people fear, the next the people hate. But when the best leader's work is done, the people say, 'We did it ourselves.'"[5]

The most effective leaders labor in relative obscurity. They don't perform for cheering crowds or adoring stockholders but simply carry out their responsibilities with humility and grace, propelling their followers to the next levels of achievement and excellence. That is essentially what a mentor does as well. I doubt there ever will be an international mentors' hall of fame, but years from now, the devoted mentor's impact will be seen and felt just the same.

I smile when I think of Dale, a man in his thirties who I have mentored for several years. An intense, detail-oriented guy, he works in a profession where you wouldn't normally expect to find someone with such a strong focus on people. But I don't think I have ever seen anyone more effective and excited about mentoring someone else. In fact, it has become such a consuming passion that he has worked hard to simplify how he works, trying to make himself both more efficient and more effective so he will have more time to spend mentoring other men.

Dale has caught the vision. When he talks in terms of "legacy," it never concerns his work, although he enjoys that immensely. He understands that his legacy — his "hundred-year vision" — is to come alongside other people, whether within or outside his company, to walk with them through their pain, to help them sift through their priorities, to show them how to discover their passions, and to assist them in becoming individuals of great character and humility. And in the process, he causes them to think about what kind of legacy they are going to have.

If Dale were to sit down across the table from you at your favorite restaurant and challenge you about the legacy your life will leave, what would you tell him?

In the next and final chapter, I have a few parting thoughts to sum up the importance of mentoring and the potential impact it can have in your life and in the lives of others. But first, once again I would like you to consider several questions.

Spanning the Legacy Gap

1. Before you started reading this chapter, if I had asked you what kind of impact your life will have one hundred years from now, how would you have responded?

2. Based on what we have just discussed, has your answer to question 1 changed? If so, how? If not, why?

3. How does the idea of reproduction — multiplying the impact of your own life through others — strike you? Can you think of any examples of this that you have witnessed or experienced personally?

4. Society typically tells us that success equates to things like money and possessions, power, position, status, achievement, and fame. Have any of those goals served as a primary motivation for you? Think about investing your life by mentoring other people who, in turn, will one day mentor others. How motivating is that idea for you?

IT'S NEVER TOO EARLY
—OR TOO LATE—TO START!

....

PRINCIPLE #10: EFFECTIVE MENTORS GO FOR IT!

....

*S*itting across the restaurant table from me was a young man in his late twenties who wanted my advice on mentoring. As he talked, I could tell that Michael had a strong desire to mentor others, not only in a workplace context but also on a personal level.

As we ate our lunch, he put down his fork, picked up a notebook and pen, and gave me a "let's get down to business" look as he prepared his question. Michael asked, "So, how do I get started in mentoring someone?" I could see the anticipation in his eyes as he waited, pen poised on paper, ready to receive some incredibly wise insights. (I felt flattered, as if I were a mentoring guru or something like that.)

I paused for a few seconds and then leaned toward him with my most serious and intense expression. "Do you really want to know how to get started?" Michael nodded as he anxiously listened for what I was about to tell him. Then I smiled and told him, "You know, I love that Nike commercial. They have really captured the essence of how to get started—'Just do it!'"

For a moment, his face went blank, and then the expression turned to shock. "That's it?" he responded. "Just do it?" "Yup," I replied. "That's it!"

To his credit, Michael took those three simple words to heart and within a month had started mentoring someone. It's a few years later and he continues to mentor others today. He accepted the fact that there is no magic formula for mentoring, no timing will ever be perfect, and no matter how uncomfortable you feel about getting started, it will never feel right until you go for it.

This has been my style for years — it's not the exception, but the rule. No one that I have invested in who now is mentoring others has ever received a lot of how-to's from me. All I offer to them are foundational principles, the same ones I have shared with you in this book. Having armed my mentoring partners with these principles, I then challenge them to think through and discover their own how-to's by turning the question around and asking them, "How do *you* think you get started in mentoring someone?"

In our society we tend to structure things to the extreme, including mentoring. This creates frustration, which results in people shying away from mentoring rather than eagerly engaging in it. You know the problem with too many how-to's? With numerous things to try to remember, our fear of making mistakes increases, and when inevitable mistakes do occur, we disengage from whatever we are doing, convincing ourselves that "I knew I couldn't do this."

That is why this book has focused on principles and big ideas. They are what count; once the principles become ingrained in us, they start to manifest themselves in everyday practice. Mentors and mentoring partners are alike; we change, not from the outside in, but from the inside out.

When I try to teach my daughter, Sarah, a new basketball technique, I understand that showing and telling her how to do it will only take her so far. She can practice it all she wants at home or in the gym, but she will never feel comfortable with this skill until she just does it, using it in a game. Even then, Sarah will have to work at executing the technique until it becomes part of her — a natural dimension of her game that doesn't require her having to constantly think about it.

The same principle holds true for mentoring. For well over a dozen years, I have conducted more leadership seminars than I can count. No matter how many how-to suggestions I offer, do you know what people still ask me when the sessions are over? "So, how do I mentor someone? What do I need to do?" They keep asking the question, "How?" I love how Peter Block reacts to this question in his excellent book *Stewardship:* "If we took responsibility for our freedom, committed ourselves to service, and had faith that our security lay within ourselves, we could stop asking the question, 'How?' We would see that we have the answer. In every case the answer to the question, 'How?' is 'Yes.' It places the location of the solution in the right place. With the questioner."[1]

Block feels so strongly about this, he even has written a new book called *The Answer to How Is Yes*. Writing specifically about mentoring, he states, "Once it [mentoring] becomes popular, a learnable skill, and an organizational project, it loses its life." Emphasizing a "go for it!" approach to mentoring, he adds, "Mentoring has meaning when we take on for ourselves the task of learning. And we do it in the face of all the help sent our way. My freedom, my purpose, my learning, all are faces of the same intention: living out my destiny and bringing this into the world with all the worth and generosity I can muster."[2]

In resisting any impulse to provide a specific how-to outline for mentoring, it's not my intent to be difficult. Actually, I want to make things easier for you. We have created such a dependency on systems, programs, and processes in every aspect of life that we have failed to realize that having too many of these how-to's can become an impediment to effectiveness. With our "to do" lists already crammed with enough tasks to fill a thirty-six-hour day, why do we want to add more pressure? Instead of me, or someone else, giving you cast-in-concrete, one-size-fits-all instructions, trust that the answers lie within you. The principles I have provided can serve as a framework, but how you mentor someone else has to come naturally, fitting your unique personality and style. So instead of expecting some kind of mentoring road map, take some time to think and reflect on what *how* looks like for you, then test your conclusions to see if they work.

There is a classic scene in the comic book–style film *Unbreakable* that I think relates well here. Actor Bruce Willis portrays David, a man desperately trying to discover who he really is and to discern his place in the world. He sees himself as just an ordinary man who works as a security guard at a university's football stadium, failing to perceive that in reality he is a superhero with unique strength and instincts for exposing criminals. (Obviously, not a true story, but hang in there with me for a moment.)

A defining moment in the film comes when David encounters Elijah (played by Samuel L. Jackson), who also happens to be seeking his rightful place in the world. By the time they meet, David already has started to realize that he is "different," mainly because he has survived several horrific catastrophes without suffering a scratch. He admits his perplexity: "I've never been injured, Elijah. What am I supposed to do?"

Elijah's answer gripped me. He tells David, "Go to where people are. You won't have to look very long. It's alright to be afraid, David. Because this part won't be like a comic book. Real life doesn't fit into little boxes that were drawn for it." Following this advice, David does go where the people are, and his eyes are finally opened. He recognizes the gifts he has and begins to use them, fulfilling his destiny of becoming a superhero.

We don't live in a comic book world, and we aren't superheroes, but the admonition applies equally for us as we contemplate mentoring opportunities — wherever people are. It *is* all right to be afraid, and real life does not fit into convenient little boxes. It's also totally acceptable not to know much about mentoring. In fact, I have observed that novice mentors often seem more effective with fewer instructions because they are forced to learn as they go. And many times that's the best way to learn.

An adage tells us, "knowledge is power," but too much knowledge can make a person arrogant and unusable. I gained some insight into this while attending a business conference held at a picturesque mountainside setting. During a break, I was talking with a retired Army major general as we gazed down to the valley below. While I had never served in the armed forces, I told him that my father had spent twenty-four years in the Army, so I had some familiarity with military life.

The veteran officer, with tears in his eyes, told me that the lofty vista we were enjoying reminded him somewhat of Vietnam. Hearing that he had commanded troops during that war, and thinking of the guys who bravely sacrificed their lives there — including some that I had known during my high school days — I asked him, "Why do we send such young men into battle?" His answer was matter-of-fact. "When you enlist young men and tell them, 'Go take that hill!' they do as you say because they don't know any better. They learn by doing. When men are older and more mature, if you tell them to take the hill, they are more apt to say something like, 'Hey, wait a second. Let's talk about this.' The more experienced you are, the less likely you are to just jump in and do as you're told."

Isn't that true? Experienced people typically ask a lot of questions. They want to know *who, what, when, why,* and *how,* analyzing everything and taking longer before actually doing what needs to be done. That's one reason I believe that, in mentoring, sometimes the less information you have the better. And the good news is that it's not nearly as hazardous as trying to capture enemy territory on foreign soil!

When I was in college, I always felt the last thing I would ever do was try to establish a career in sales. But four years after I had graduated from college, what profession did I find myself in? Sales. I didn't like the idea of having to deal with rejection. If it had been up to me, the customers would have just lined up outside my door and I would have cordially taken their orders one by one. Of course, the industry does not work that way. Potential customers for the medical products I sold were out there in hospitals and doctors' offices, and I had to go to them, risking rejection every time I walked through a door.

I received extensive training, but no matter how thoroughly my company trained me, I felt certain it was not enough. Along with the training, I received ample encouragement from other sales representatives and even traveled for two weeks, night and day, with a seasoned sales mentor. But training and encouragement could only take me to a certain point. The time came when I just had to get out there and do it, making real the principles and techniques I had learned. I encountered my share of failures — and I didn't like it — but even while failing, I still gained from those experiences and gradually became more effective. This helped me in mentoring because I realized that the only way to take the first step was just to go for it, instead of merely thinking and talking about it.

When Anne was pregnant with our first child, like many young couples we sought the counsel of other people. Determined that we didn't want to make mistakes, we asked questions about how to effectively raise children. We got lots of good insight and advice from people who had years and years of child-rearing experience. But you know what? Once our son was born, all that wonderful counsel we had received didn't matter. It seemed as if everything went blank; the baby had arrived and suddenly we had the awesome and sometimes overwhelming responsibility of taking care of him.

Despite tremendous advice and our prenatal training, we still felt woefully inadequate for the task — and yes, we made plenty of mistakes. You might say we didn't know what we didn't know. If you have children of your own, you understand what I mean. Regardless, there was no turning back; we had to learn — sometimes on the fly. At times it even seemed like our infant Paul was the teacher!

Comparing this to mentoring, remember that people are unique, just as babies are unique, and no two mentoring relationships are alike. Even if there were some sort of mentoring mold out there somewhere, you would have to throw it away because it wouldn't fit the next person you mentor.

We could extend these comparisons to getting ready for marriage or receiving an education to get a good job. Preparation and instruction is never sufficient for dealing with the day-to-day realities of marriage and career. The best thing is to proceed, do it, and learn along the way.

You get the point. Getting started in mentoring is not so much a matter of how-to as it is a question of whether you are willing and available to come alongside someone and offer whatever help you can for that person to become all that he or she is designed to be. Are you willing to go for it?

FINDING MENTORING PARTNERS

Often people ask where they can find prospective mentoring partners, as if partners are needles in some humongous haystack. I assure them that opportunities are all around us, and we'll see them if we're just willing to look. I also offer the same advice that the Bruce Willis character received in *Unbreakable:* "You won't have to look very long." When opportunity knocks, the most practical thing you can do is answer the door.

S. Truett Cathy, founder and chairman of Chick-fil-A, the highly successful and innovative fast-food chain, makes a similar observation in his newest book, *Eat Mor Chikin, Inspire More People:*

> The lesson that is continually reinforced in me is that to take advantage of unexpected opportunities, we must leave ourselves available. If we had set lofty long-range goals for our company's growth, our capital might have been so tied up in construction that we would have been unable to respond to these opportunities.
>
> Many successful people I know set magnificent goals for themselves, then let nothing stand in the way of achievement. I don't engage in that type of long-range planning. Instead, I leave myself and my company available to take advantage of opportunities as they arise.

I'm not suggesting that we wander aimlessly waiting for opportunities to drop out of the sky. We commit ourselves to a purpose, and we don't overcommit our resources. That way of thinking has allowed us to grow steadily into a billion-dollar business with 1,000 restaurants while responding to the needs around us.[3]

Applying this wisdom to mentoring, we must leave ourselves available and try to recognize opportunities around us when they present themselves. Is it a little scary? Sure, but almost anything worth doing seems a bit intimidating the first time you try it. Think about all the life experiences you have accumulated and about how much you have to share with others. Someone well deserving would like to be the beneficiary of what life has taught you. That "someone" could be sitting in the next cubicle, in the office down the hall, or across the street.

Let's suppose you are thinking, "Okay, I'm willing. I'm available. I'm going to keep my eyes open for opportunities. But where are they? I don't recall running into anyone lately who was just begging to be mentored!" Let me give you some suggestions for some great places to look for mentoring opportunities.

Families first. First and foremost, the best place to start is with your own family. As I admonish would-be mentors, "If it's not working at home, don't be a hypocrite and take it outside the home." I also point out that the home is by far the best learning laboratory. The principles we have discussed in this book easily relate to marriage and family life, and applying them in the home can provide great experience as we prepare to mentor people outside the home.

Anne and I have applied these principles with each other and in raising our children, and the results have been absolutely incredible.

I would highly recommend them for any family, even those with teenagers — especially those with teenagers!

Nonprofits. This may be the safest learning laboratory of all. Volunteering in a nonprofit organization leaves a lot of room for you to take risks, experiment with new things, and even fail. One professional journal pointed out that the majority of CEOs developed their best leadership skills while volunteering for nonprofit organizations.

There are so many of these, you can afford to pick and choose which one you would like to work with the most. It could be one that you are already giving money to, because that is where some of your passions lie. Inquire and see if they have mentoring opportunities available, letting them know of your interest. You can find nonprofit mentoring opportunities by visiting the Web sites of other organizations that interest you. You also might discover them at your place of worship, a youth group, or a university.

My initial mentoring experience came through a nonprofit, so I think this area is particularly promising. As I suggest to people I have mentored and coached, nonprofits can provide a "second track" when they feel stuck in jobs that don't fulfill their passions.

One reason I call nonprofits "safe" places to mentor is because you can quit at any time if the experience fails to meet your expectations. Some nonprofits, wanting to maintain a level of stability among their workers — paid and unpaid — ask for commitments of up to eighteen months, but don't let them put you on a guilt trip. It's your time and energy, and if you find the experience fulfilling you will want to stay on, probably a lot longer than eighteen months. But if the experience isn't what you were looking for, you need to be free to seek a more suitable place for mentoring. Commitment must come from *your* heart, not the nonprofit's.

Craig, a young man I was mentoring, developed into an excellent mentor within about a year's time, largely because he was already involved in an organization that works with teenagers in the inner city. He was able to take the principles he learned through our relationship and apply them in mentoring young people. In modeling what life-changing mentoring looks like, Craig became an inspiration for others to follow.

The young people have benefited enormously, the experience for him has been invaluable, and now these principles have infiltrated his approach to everything he does at work. In addition, peers at his company have felt drawn to Craig and want him to mentor them because of qualities they admire in him. Essentially, this is why Leader's Legacy exists. We are striving to develop a network of people who want to learn how to mentor others and who in turn will become mentors themselves.

Friends and neighbors. Tell your friends or neighbors of your interest in mentoring people. After more than twenty-three years of mentoring, I have yet to exhaust the available resource of friends. This is partly because mentoring relationships often spawn other relationships. For instance, on some occasions I have started to mentor the sons of men who I had the privilege of investing in years before.

Your workplace. While this is a very fertile field for finding mentoring prospects, it is the most sensitive of the areas I have mentioned. It is important for executives to develop their people, and the principles in this book will be a great help in understanding how to address the "whole" person. However, as Block points out in *The Answer to How Is Yes,* "don't look to your boss to be a mentor. . . . Your boss may be a great mentor, but your boss has power over you, and this gives an edge to the guidance offered. And if you want to fire your boss as a mentor, you have to do it indirectly and with diffi-culty."[4] He suggests finding someone to mentor — or to mentor you — who can do so free of any supervisory entanglements.

If you do mentor people who work for you, assure them of how committed you are to them, but also explain that if it should become necessary for you to fire them one day, you could not let the mentor-ing relationship stand in the way. Mentoring and working relation-ships need to be handled independently. Many CEOs I talk with desire to build a "family" corporate culture, a very commendable value that can be established. However, because a mentoring relationship should never be allowed to interfere with fair and equitable business practices, it could become an obstacle to being able to mentor as fully and deeply as needed.

When mentoring in the workplace, the best advice is to find some-one in a different department where there is not a direct reporting rela-tionship. Don't make things more complicated than they need to be.

WHERE WOULD I BE TODAY?

Occasionally, I wonder what would have been different for me if I had never been mentored. For one thing, I'm sure many of the issues I wrestled with as a young adult — my career, finances, relationships, purpose and direction for my life — would have taken much longer to resolve, if they had gotten resolved at all. Messes take a lot longer to clean up when you have to do it all by yourself. I may have never acquired the strong zeal for mentoring that I have today. Thankfully, I don't have to speculate about that. But if you've never been men-tored, don't let that stop you from mentoring others.

This has been the case for Stan, a good friend of mine. After graduating from college, he basically had to find his own way once he started a career. Some people came along to help with professional expertise, but there was no one whose special role was just to "be there" for him, to listen and guide him over the bumps of life. Despite this, Stan shows as much enthusiasm for mentoring as anyone I know.

He explains it this way: "I really wish someone had been available for me in my twenties, when I was busy making some of the biggest mistakes of my life. I think a mentor could have helped me avoid at least some of them, so I — and others — could have been spared considerable pain. But frankly, that makes me more determined to mentor others. Recognizing how much it would have meant for me, I want to make sure that through me at least a few others receive the help and support I didn't even realize at the time that I needed."

DON'T SET YOUR SIGHTS TOO HIGH

Hopefully, as you have reflected on our principles of mentoring, your excitement has grown and expanded. Perhaps you are champing at the proverbial bit, ready to go. I certainly don't want to temper your enthusiasm, but let me suggest that when you start mentoring, it is always best to start small.

Begin with just one person to mentor. Whether you are a CEO with multiple employees, a leader in a nonprofit organization, or a line employee, you can model these principles by building into the life of just one person. The greatest movements had the smallest of beginnings.

Take Jesus, for example, whom I consider the best example there is. He invested three full years with only twelve men, being with them around the clock, day after day. Even then, his success rate was not 100 percent, as one man ended up betraying him. But look at the impact Jesus has had on our world today, many centuries later. That should give us inspiration. Even individual efforts, once they multiply, can have impacts far beyond anything we can imagine.

Also, don't have high expectations for yourself or the person you mentor. Model humility with your first mentoring partner, acknowledging that you are new at this. Don't claim expertise that you don't have. Your honesty will be appreciated. Hope for the best, but if the relationship fails, don't give up. As Thomas Edison pursued his vision of the light bulb, every failure brought him that much closer to success. Almost everyone fails the first time they try something new, whether it involves riding a bicycle or mentoring — but how else are you going to learn?

A WORD FOR OLDER MENTORS

One of the great tragedies of our society is that people quit being productive long before they should, as if the term *retirement* means "nothing of value left to give." Nothing could be further from the truth. I have already mentioned several men I know who are in their seventies or eighties and continue to have strong influence in the lives of others, and I can think of dozens of other examples.

Recently, someone reminded me of the example of John Glenn, who in 1962 made history with his manned orbital flight around the earth. He later went on to become a U.S. senator. As he advanced into his seventies, Glenn could have rested on his laurels, written his memoirs, and just reflected on his accomplishments. But at the age of seventy-eight, when many of his contemporaries were scheduling their next round of golf, he decided another trip into outer space would be fitting. As radio commentator Ron Hutchcraft said, "At a time when a lot of people think all their important missions are behind them, John Glenn was still flying them!"

If you have been eligible for a senior citizen's discount for a while, you have probably experienced (and survived) more than your share of battles in the workplace—and elsewhere. Maybe you feel you have earned a rest, but think of the storehouse of wisdom and experience you have accumulated. Don't hoard it—find opportunities to share it and, in the process, discover how you will gain all the more.

Wouldn't it be a wonderful legacy to have it said of you that up to the very last you kept giving and giving—showing others how to do the same? Don't use time as an excuse. You don't have time *not* to mentor. The time to start is ... well, yesterday. It does not matter where you are in life or how old you are. There are no age qualifications or barriers for mentoring.

THINGS CHANGE—SO EXPECT IT!

One final admonition about the importance of clinging to fundamental principles, rather than arbitrary how-to's: As we all know, we live in a world of unprecedented change. Sometimes changes occur on the magnitude of a 9-11, when instantly it seems the world has turned upside down. Other times the changes are far more subtle; they may not be tragic in any sense, but they are significant just the same. In a dynamic world, located in a dynamic universe, and working with dynamic people, we need to understand that things change constantly—even methods.

The years following the Industrial Revolution made life relatively simple. It was "command and control"—those in charge gave the orders and everyone followed them. The rules of business and life are vastly different today, and when you engage with people, the command-and-control model doesn't work anymore — at least not in the long term.

To survive and succeed in the twenty-first century, we need to become accustomed to ambiguity, uncertainty, continual change, and transition. This applies to all of life — even mentoring. So instead of looking for a formula or method for mentoring that may seem right for the moment, simply hang onto the principles and adjust the rules and procedures as you go to fit your personality and style.

I hope what I have shared from my own life and experience has whetted your appetite for more, preparing you for what I am certain could become the greatest adventure of your life. What happens may absolutely amaze you.

I hope you will find the courage to *go for it!*

Some Final Questions Before You Go for It

1. How comfortable are you about entering into a mentoring relationship without a how-to guideline to follow?

2. As you look at the people around you — in your home, your neighborhood, your workplace — can you envision any of them as someone you could mentor (or be mentored by)? If so, how might you pursue this opportunity?

3. If I were to tell you to "Just do it!" or "Go for it!" and get involved in mentoring as soon as possible, what — if anything — might stop you?

TEN POWERFUL PRINCIPLES FOR
EFFECTIVE MENTORING

1. Effective mentors understand that living is about giving.

2. Effective mentors see mentoring as a process that requires perseverance.

3. Effective mentors open their world to their mentoring partners.

4. Effective mentors help mentoring partners align passion and work.

5. Effective mentors are comforters who share the load.

6. Effective mentors help turn personal values into practice.

7. Effective mentors model character.

8. Effective mentors affirm the value of spirituality.

9. Effective mentors recognize that
   Mentoring + Reproduction = Legacy.

10. Effective mentors go for it!

NOTES

CHAPTER 1: IT STARTS WITH THE HEART

1. Peter Block, *Stewardship* (San Francisco, Calif.: Berrett-Koehler Publishers, 1996), p. 10.

CHAPTER 2: IT'S THE JOURNEY THAT COUNTS

1. Peter Senge, *The Fifth Discipline* (New York: Doubleday, 1994), p. 345.

CHAPTER 3: INTO THEIR WORLD—THROUGH YOURS

1. David A. Thomas, "The Truth About Mentoring Minorities: Race Matters," *Harvard Business Review*, vol. 79, no. 4 (April 2001), p. 104.

2. Robert K. Cooper, *Executive EQ: Emotional Intelligence in Leadership and Organizations* (New York: Grosset/Putnam Publishers, 1997), p. 68.

3. Cooper, p. 71.

4. Bill Thrall, Bruce McNicol, and Ken McElrath, *The Ascent of a Leader* (San Francisco: Jossey-Bass, 1999), p. 81.

5. Douglas A. Ready, "How Storytelling Builds Next-Generation Leaders," *MIT Sloan Management Review*, vol. 43, no. 4 (Summer 2002), p. 64.

CHAPTER 4: ADDRESSING THE DESIRES OF THE HEART

1. Quoted in William D. Hitt, ed., *Thoughts on Leadership: A Treasury of*

Quotations (Columbus, Ohio: Battelle Press, 1992), p. 202.

2. Hitt, p. 79.

3. Roger Birkman, *True Colors* (Nashville, Tenn.: Thomas Nelson, 1995), p. 58.

4. Roger Lewin and Birute Regine, *The Soul at Work* (New York: Simon & Schuster, 2000), p. 327.

5. Birkman International, Inc., is based in Houston, Texas. For more information on the Birkman Method personal assessment resources, visit their Web site, www.birkman.com

CHAPTER 5: ADVANCING THROUGH ADVERSITY

1. Dr. Paul Brand and Philip Yancey, *Pain: The Gift Nobody Wants* (New York: HarperCollins, 1993), p. 13.

2. David Chadwick, *The 12 Leadership Principles of Dean Smith* (Kingston, N.Y.: Total/Sports Illustrated, 1999), p. 41.

3. Jane E. Dutton, et al., "Leading in Times of Trauma," *Harvard Business Review*, vol. 80, no. 1 (January 2002), pp. 55-57.

4. Dutton, p. 58.

5. See Viktor Emil Frankl, *Man's Search for Meaning* (New York: Simon & Schuster, 1984).

CHAPTER 6: LET YOUR VALUES FILTER BE YOUR GUIDE

1. Frances Hesselbein, ed., *The Drucker Foundation: The Leader of the Future* (San Francisco: Jossey-Bass, 1995), p. 103.

2. Diane Brady, "Rethinking the Rat Race," *Business Week*, 26 Aug. 2002, p. 142.

CHAPTER 7: THE SUBSTANCE OF MENTORING

1. Jim Collins, "Level 5 Leadership: The Triumph of Humility and Firm

Resolve," *Harvard Business Review*, vol. 79, no. 1 (January 2001), pp. 68-73. (Collins' findings have since been expanded into his book *Good to Great*, Harper Business, 2001.)

2. Os Guinness, *When No One Sees: The Importance of Character in an Age of Image* (Colorado Springs, Colo.: NavPress, 2000), p. 187.

CHAPTER 8: THE FUEL THAT DRIVES THE ENGINE

1. Michelle Conlin, "Religion in the Workplace," *Business Week*, 1 Nov. 1999, pp. 150-158.

2. Survey, "How Do You Stack Up?" *Redbook*, vol. 199, no. 2 (August 2002), p. 100.

3. Gerald L. Schroeder, *The Hidden Face of God* (New York: Simon & Schuster, 2002), pp. 8-9.

4. Marc Gunther, "God and Business," *FORTUNE*, vol. 144, no. 1 (9 July 2001), p. 64.

5. Ian I. Mitroff and Elizabeth A. Penton, "A Study of Spirituality in the Workplace," *MIT Sloan Management Review*, vol. 40, no. 4 (Summer 1999), p. 88.

6. Jim Loehr and Tony Schwartz, "The Making of a Corporate Athlete," *Harvard Business Review*, vol. 79, no. 1 (January 2001), p. 128.

CHAPTER 9: THE VISION GAP: FOCUSING ON THE FUTURE

1. John P. Kotter, *Leading Change* (Boston: Harvard Business School Publishing, 1996), pp. 68-69.

2. Chuck Salter, "Enough Is Enough," *Fast Company* 26 (August 1999), p. 122.

3. Max DePree, *Leading Without Power* (San Francisco: Jossey-Bass, 1997), pp. 174-175.

4. Stephen Covey, *The 7 Habits of Highly Effective People* (New York: Simon & Schuster, 1990), p. 95.

5. Quoted in Lewis D. Eigen and Jonathan P. Siegel, *The Manager's Book of Quotations* (Rockville, Md.: The Quotation Corporation, 1989), p. 222.

CHAPTER 10: IT'S NEVER TOO EARLY—OR TOO LATE—TO START!

1. Peter Block, *Stewardship: Choose Service over Self-Interest* (San Francisco: Berrett-Koehler Publishers, 1996), p. 235.

2. Peter Block, *The Answer to How Is Yes* (San Francisco: Berrett-Koehler Publishers, 2001), pp. 101-103.

3. S. Truett Cathy, *Eat Mor Chikin, Inspire More People* (Decatur, Ga.: Looking Glass Books, 2002), pp. 4-5.

4. Block, *The Answer to How Is Yes*, pp. 101-103.

ABOUT THE AUTHOR

*D*avid A. Stoddard is founder and president of Leader's Legacy, Inc., a not-for-profit organization that focuses on developing leaders through specialized training, executive coaching, and mentoring. A graduate of San Diego State University, he built a successful career in sales and marketing in the healthcare industry before joining the leadership team of a nonprofit organization in 1991. Dave has been involved in personal mentoring for more than twenty years. He and his wife, Anne, live in suburban Atlanta with their daughter and two sons.

LEADER'S LEGACY, INC.

Leader's Legacy, Inc. provides an intensive, value-added mentoring/coaching process for developing people, both personally and professionally, from the inside out. Founded in 2000 by David A. Stoddard in Atlanta, Georgia, Leader's Legacy is working to establish a network of mentors across the United States and around the world who understand and model the principles for developing people for sustained life-changing results.

For more information about Leader's Legacy and the "Heart of Mentoring" process for developing leaders, please visit the following web sites:

www.leaderslegacy.com

www.theheartofmentoring.com

"Being mentored through Leader's Legacy has been life-changing. It has grounded me, helping me to learn how to focus on what's really important, understanding how to put things in my life and career in proper perspective."

Brad Thomas, Attorney
Warshauer, Woodruff, & Thomas, P.C.

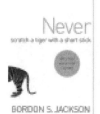